Gustav Klimt
Masterpieces of Art

Publisher and Creative Director: Nick Wells
Senior Project Editor and Picture Research: Catherine Taylor
Art Director: Mike Spender
Copy Editor: Ramona Lamport
Proofreader: Dawn Laker

Special thanks to: Robert Zakes and Emma Chafer.

FLAME TREE PUBLISHING

Crabtree Hall, Crabtree Lane
Fulham, London SW6 6TY
United Kingdom

www.flametreepublishing.com

First published 2014

14 16 18 17 15
1 3 5 7 9 10 8 6 4 2

A CIP record for this book is available from the British Library upon request.

Image credits: Courtesy of **akg-images**: 88. © **Artothek**: 31, 42, 44, 55, 61, 62, 73, 77, 84, 99, 106, 107, 109, 114; and the following: Blauel/Gnamm 59; IMAGNO 53, 45, 56, 57, 60, 78, 90, 87, 89, 111, 125, 93; Jochen Remmer 79, 91, 115; Christie's Images Ltd 80, 76, 85, 92, 103, 112; Hans Hinz 117. © 2014 **Scala, Florence**: 119; and the following: Austrian Archives 38, Fine Art Images/Heritage Images 64. Courtesy of **Superstock**: 100; and the following: DeAgostini 30, 32, 35, 36, 58, 65, 68, 70, 75, 83, 96, 97, 108, 120, 122, 124; Fine Art Images 33, 34, 37, 39, 43, 47, 48, 50, 69, 71, 72, 81, 82, 98, 101, 102, 104, 110, 113, 121; Universal Images Group 46, 52, 105; Buyenlarge 54, 116, 118; Image Asset Management Ltd 63; Bridgeman Art Library 74; Lucas Vallecillos 86, 123.

Hardback ISBN 978-1-78361-139-3
Paperback ISBN 978-1-78361-260-4

Printed in China

Gustav Klimt
Masterpieces of Art

Susie Hodge

FLAME TREE
PUBLISHING

Contents

Gustav Klimt:
The Pursuit of Beauty

One of the founders of the Vienna Secession movement and often regarded as the greatest painter of the Art Nouveau period, Gustav Klimt (1862–1918) was born in Baumgarten, a suburb of Vienna, the second of seven children. His father, Ernst Klimt (1834–92), was of Moravian peasant stock, his mother Anna (1836–1915), was Viennese. Ernst Klimt was an engraver and goldsmith, but he struggled to support his family, particularly after the Viennese stock market crash of 1873.

In addition to financial hardships, tragedy struck the family in 1874 when, at the age of five, Klimt's younger sister Anna died after a long illness and, soon after, his sister Klara suffered a mental breakdown. For the rest of his life, Klimt worried about his health and possible hereditary madness.

'Gesamtkunstwerk'

While still at school, Gustav and his two younger brothers Ernst (1864–92) and Georg (1867–1931) demonstrated precocious art and craft skills. In recognition of his talents, when he was fourteen, a relative encouraged Klimt to take the entrance examination for the Kunstgewerbeschule, the Viennese School of Applied Art. The Kunstgewerbeschule had opened in 1867 as a less exalted version of the Vienna Academy of Fine Arts. Emulating the school of the South Kensington Museum in London, it aimed to replace the apprenticeship system that had been adversely affected by industrialization, and to prepare its students to either design for industry or to teach. The principal of the school, Rudolf Eitelberger von Edelberg (1817–85), was inspired by the English Arts and Crafts movement, believing that equality should be afforded to all art forms, and that crafts should be as highly respected as painting, sculpture and architecture. Eitelberger's belief that all art forms should be united in a comprehensive 'Gesamtkunstwerk' (total art work) later became one of the key principles of international Art Nouveau. The Kunstgewerbeschule was divided into four departments: architecture, figural drawing and painting, decorative drawing and painting, and sculpture.

Exceptional Talent

Klimt believed that the wide range of techniques taught at the Kunstgewerbeschule would help him to become a drawing instructor. He passed the entrance exam with distinction and, with the help of an official grant, worked diligently for seven years from 1876 to 1883, studying historical and technical aspects of the Arts and Crafts movement and a range of skills including mosaic, fresco, painting, and especially the disciplined copying of other artists' work. After he had completed the introductory coursework, he prepared to take the qualifying exam to become a teacher, but Professor Eitelberger had noticed his extraordinary talent and advised him to abandon thoughts of teaching, encouraging him instead to join the department of figural drawing and painting. Exceptionally gifted students were also selected to attend Professor Ferdinand Julius Laufberger's (1829–81) classes in decorative drawing and painting, which were as outstanding as any lessons offered by the Academy of Fine Arts. With his exemplary talents and application, Klimt was selected to study with Professor Laufberger.

Magician of Colours

The following year, Klimt's younger brother Ernst, and their friend Franz Matsch (1861–1942), enrolled at the Kunstgewerbeschule, and a year later Georg Klimt also enrolled. Gustav, Ernst and Matsch worked so well together that, even while they were still studying, their professors, including Eitelberger, Laufberger and Michael Rieser (1828–1905), secured them several paid commissions. In 1879, they worked on designs for Festzug, a pageant that was organized for the whole of Vienna to celebrate the silver wedding anniversary of Emperor Franz Joseph (1830–1916) and Empress Elisabeth (1837–98). The director of this project was Hans Makart (1840–84), a leading contemporary Viennese painter who enjoyed celebrity status and painted huge decorative canvases evoking the vitality and fluidity of Peter Paul Rubens (1577–1640) and the vivid colours of the late-fifteenth-century Venetian School. Also a designer of flamboyant interiors, Makart was nicknamed the 'magician of colours'. Klimt especially revered him, particularly for his use of dramatic effects of light, symbolism and brilliant colours, and dreamed of emulating Makart's success. 'Makartstil', or Makart style, later came to be seen as the basis for Jugendstil ('Youth Style'), the Austrian Art Nouveau style that developed within a few years.

Allegories and Emblems

Hundreds of students, including Klimt, worked with Makart on floats for the Festzug procession, which later became known as the 'Makart Parade'. In 1880, Gustav, Ernst and Matsch collaborated on allegories for the Palais Sturany, a private house in Vienna, and on a ceiling

painting for the thermal baths in Carlsbad. Klimt also received some lucrative commissions of his own, the most important from the publisher Martin Gerlach, who invited the nineteen-year-old Klimt to contribute illustrations for a set of three books called *Allegories and Emblems* (*see* pages 30 and 31), which provided models for artists to use when preparing their own historical or allegorical paintings. The

in 1883, the three artists opened their own studio in Vienna, and formed the 'Künstlercompagnie der Gebrüder Klimt und Matsch' (The Company of Artists, Klimt Brothers and Matsch), which immediately began profiting from the building boom of the Ringstrasse Era.

The Ringstrasse Era

The Ringstrasse Era was a period in Vienna that began in 1857 and lasted until the outbreak of the First World War in 1914. It began when Franz Joseph ordered the destruction of the ancient fortifications that had surrounded the medieval city centre, and in their place authorized the construction of the 'Ringstrasse,' a magnificent boulevard that encircled the centre of the city, lined with stately buildings and beautiful parks. For more than 30 years, as the Ringstrasse was being constructed, the city was full of workmen, bricks, dust and scaffolding.

Among the buildings, Franz Joseph commissioned two monumental museums to be built near his palace, one dedicated to the arts – the Kunsthistorisches Museum – and the other to the natural sciences – the Naturhistorisches Museum. There was also a church built in imitation of Cologne Cathedral, the parliament, a town hall, a stock exchange, a courthouse, a university, a new theatre, a state opera house and numerous other public buildings, as well as 650 houses, apartment blocks and hotels. Those who could afford to live there displayed their wealth in fancy façades and opulent interiors, and the entire building programme of the Ringstrasse generated countless possibilities for artists. The Künstlercompagnie was introduced, probably by Professor Laufberger, to various influential people, including the renowned architectural firm of Fellner and Helmer that specialized in building theatres.

Austria and Hungary United

In 1867, Austria and Hungary had united under Franz Joseph's leadership, and for the first time in history a law was passed to make all Austro-Hungarian citizens equal. As a result, Vienna's population rapidly expanded, as many migrated to the city from across the empire. By the turn of the twentieth century, Vienna had two million inhabitants and was the fourth largest city in Europe. It witnessed a cultural

books attempted to rekindle the myth and symbolism of Renaissance and Baroque art, and for some of his eleven allegorical contributions Klimt emulated his hero Makart's style. On completion of their studies

evolution unparalleled anywhere else at that time, as the wealthy citizens immersed themselves in the arts and surrounded themselves with splendour. Many of the newly arrived families had amassed fortunes from industry and trade, and a number of them commissioned Klimt and his partners.

Predominantly, however, the Künstlercompagnie was given work by Fellner and Helmer. As a result, throughout the 1880s, the three young men were greatly in demand, designing interiors either privately for the rich or particularly for theatres all over the empire. Some of their earliest and most ambitious projects were ceiling paintings and decorative frescoes for the Romanian National Theatre in Bucharest, and paintings in the Municipal Theatre of Fiume in Croatia.

Villa Hermes

In 1885, the Künstlercompagnie was given the important job of decorating the Empress Elisabeth's country retreat, the Villa Hermes, just outside Vienna. There they executed large paintings illustrating scenes from Shakespeare's *A Midsummer Night's Dream*. This was their first significant imperial commission and it brought them to the attention of the Emperor and his favourite architect, Karl von Hasenauer (1833–94), who had built the Villa Hermes. In preparation for every project, Klimt researched and collected a great deal of information from which he developed his ideas. In their exacting interpretations of classical and historical themes, the three artists conformed to the expectations of both the public and the official art bodies in Vienna.

The Burgtheater

Hasenauer had witnessed the Künstlercompagnie's exhaustive research and scrupulous application at the Villa Hermes, and he was probably responsible for their first major Viennese assignment: a cycle of paintings for the tympanum and two staircase ceilings of the newly constructed Burgtheater, the Austrian National Theatre (1878–88). Built by Hasenauer, it was one of the most important buildings in the Ringstrasse development, and the trio's most prestigious commission to date. They did not have to conceive the decorative programme

themselves, but use their imaginations in following a brief. The theme was the development of the theatre from its beginnings in ancient Greece, and the artists divided the work between them. Klimt painted *The Chariot of Thespian*, *Shakespeare's Globe Theatre*, *The Altar of Dionysius*, *The Theatre in Taormina* (see page 32) and *The Altar of Venus*, while Ernst and Matsch were responsible for five other scenes.

As with their other projects, their Burgtheater paintings were created from painstaking historical research and attention to detail. In their pursuit of accuracy, the artists read widely, studied in museums, hired costumes or had them made, and used friends, family and professional models to pose for each figure featured. With his outstanding skills, Klimt supplemented the expected classical motifs in his paintings with exceptionally realistic portraits, painted with precision and astonishing technical skill. The Künstlercompagnie took two years to complete the commission, and in 1888 the Emperor awarded them the Goldene

Verdienstkreuz (the Golden Order of Merit) for the work. Wide public acclaim followed and Klimt was also made an honorary member of the Universities of Munich and Vienna. Secretly, however, he was rather

disappointed with himself. He had intended to break new ground with his paintings and to be noticed for being different, not to have conformed so closely to expectations.

Academic Art

In the first half of the nineteenth century a new market for art developed across Europe. Patrons came not only from the highest ranks of society as they always had done, but now also from the increasingly prosperous middle classes. The art trade was established through official exhibitions, dealers and mass-produced prints. Artists trained in accredited academies, focusing on refining their drawing skills. They were expected to represent the human form realistically, following accurate imitations of classical forms in natural-looking poses.

Colour had also recently gained importance, and the artists who enjoyed the greatest acclaim amalgamated accurate, sensitive drawing with the use of vibrant colour. In the 1880s in Vienna, this highly realistic style known as academic art was considered the most admirable of all artistic approaches. French artists such as Théodore Chassériau (1819–56), Thomas Couture (1815–79) and William-Adolphe Bouguereau (1825–1905) were particularly esteemed, while newer developments in art were virtually ignored.

Historicism and Hierarchy

Historicism corresponded with academic art and was applied to both art and design by the end of the nineteenth century. It was used in modern works of artistic styles from earlier periods. In painting, historical styles were used to portray the era that the painting depicted as authentically as possible; in design, historicism could be expressed through form, techniques and materials. Architecture in the Ringstrasse exploited historicism. For instance, the Parliament was built in the Hellenistic style, following the belief that the government in classical Athens was the original, truest form of democracy. The City Hall was in Neogothic style, to imitate the successful self-government of Flanders. The Votivkirche was built in the French Gothic style, and the University of Vienna replicated buildings of the Italian Renaissance.

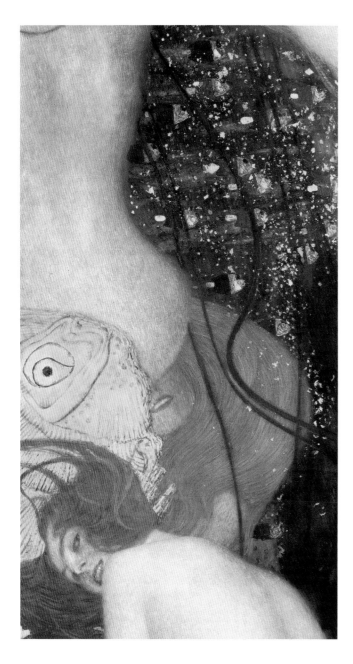

Meanwhile, a hierarchy of subjects had become established within the art world, with some being considered more worthy than others. History painting – including myths, religious, classical, literary or allegorical subjects – was regarded as the most eminent, and was often called the 'grande genre'. Next came portraits, where close likenesses were greatly admired, especially if the artist expressed the sitter's personality. Following portraiture came genre painting, or scenes of everyday life, while lower down the scale came landscape, and finally still life.

Evolving Style

It was against this strict background of stylistic expectations that Klimt had grown up and had become a professional artist. While he had conformed to, and excelled at, the styles of painting expected of him, he was also aware that many artists elsewhere had rebelled against orthodoxy and were breaking away from academic art and official stipulations. For instance, in France, the Realists, Impressionists and Symbolists were creating colourful, nonconformist works. Klimt was of the same generation as Edvard Munch (1863–1944), Wassily Kandinsky (1866–1944) and Henri Matisse (1869–1954), who in their own countries were each breaking new artistic ground.

In painting public buildings in elegant, cultured Vienna at the end of the nineteenth century, Klimt was obliged to conform. Yet in view of the Viennese love of grandeur and elaboration, he believed that decoration and ornamentation could become more flamboyant. While many of his contemporaries were vigorously against this notion, he began to develop new ideas, drawing on several influences, including his father's goldsmith work, Makart's paintings, evolving ideas of Art Nouveau and Symbolism, and from his research for other commissioned paintings he took elements from ancient Egyptian, Greek and Eastern art.

The Old Burgtheater

Even though he was disappointed in his work at the Burgtheater, the paintings Klimt produced for it were a decisive factor in his next important commission. In 1887, Matsch and he were asked by the City Council of Vienna to make a record of the Old Burgtheater that was to be demolished the following year. Klimt's subsequent painting, *The Auditorium in the Old Burgtheater* (1888–89, *see* page 33), portrayed the interior of the auditorium unusually from the stage rather than from the audience's viewpoint. Among nearly two hundred prominent members of Viennese society that he included in the audience as tiny portraits were politicians, scientists, artists and society beauties, including the

The Kunsthistorisches Museum

In 1890, the Künstlercompagnie also received another significant commission, the decoration of the imposing entrance hall of the Kunsthistorisches Museum (the Museum of Art History, or the Museum of Fine Arts), which housed the imperial art collections. Makart had originally been commissioned to carry out the work, but it had been left unfinished after his premature death in 1884. Although the older and more established artist Mihály Munkácsy (1844–1900) was employed to continue Makart's work on the ceiling, the Klimt brothers and Matsch were to paint the more difficult, awkwardly shaped spandrels on the ceiling and the spaces between the marble columns on the walls. They were to represent the development of art from the ancient Egyptian and Greek to the Rococo era. Before starting, they determined, by drawing lots, which period and country each would work on, and once again, after comprehensive research, they produced highly finished, sumptuous paintings. Klimt painted eleven of the works and, although all three artists attempted to make their painting styles similar enough to look coherent, for the first time, Klimt's work was beginning to surpass that of his partners.

Personal Tragedy

The Künstlercompagnie was by now so successful that, in 1892, the three young men were able to move to a larger studio in the Josephstadt district, closer to the centre of Vienna. Their prospects seemed to be assured. Then Klimt suffered a double tragedy when his father died at the age of 58, and six months later, at just 28 years, his brother Ernst died of pericarditis following a heavy cold.

Grief stricken, Klimt assumed financial responsibility for his mother, sisters and Ernst's young wife and infant daughter and, from that time, depression, which also affected his mother and sister Klara, became a recurrent feature in his life. However, he soon became intimate with a young woman who would be his lifelong companion and support. Ernst's widow Helene Flöge was from a middle-class family, and Klimt became a frequent guest at their homes in the city and the countryside. There he met Helene's sister, the elegant and intelligent Emilie Flöge.

composers Johannes Brahms (1833–97) and Karl Goldmark (1830–1915) and the Emperor's mistress, the actress Katharina Schratt. When it was discovered that Karl Lueger, later Mayor of Vienna, was not there, Klimt added him. He made over 1,500 preparatory sketches for the painting, and the lifelike accuracy yet apparent spontaneity of the final work met with great public approval. In 1890, he was awarded the Kaiserpreis (Emperor's Prize) for the painting, and the ensuing society portraits he was commissioned to paint confirmed his position as the most fashionable portraitist of the day.

Romantic Life

Klimt was exceptionally close to his mother and sisters (he remained living with them for most of his life), and had numerous female friends and lovers, but he never married. Even his earliest art shows a highly developed appreciation of the female form and throughout his life he painted the female nude for his own pleasure as well as in preparation for his large allegorical paintings. Yet his relationships with women continue to baffle critics and historians.

It is known that Klimt had numerous affairs, especially with his models, and that he fathered at least 14 illegitimate children. His many relationships with women were frequently intimate, but they were not always sexual. Although he still conducted many sexual affairs while with Emilie Flöge, his relationship with her almost certainly remained platonic. Many of his works display sexual taboos, which were the subject of much gossip in Vienna at the time, and have given rise to various theories and debates, but, without direct explanations from Klimt himself, the rationale behind them remains obscure. Also ambiguous are many of the names of the women in his life, partly because Emilie burnt much of his correspondence after his death. Throughout his life, he kept his affairs discreet and avoided personal scandal, but when he died some of his models began legal proceedings to establish that he was the father of their children. The legal rights of just four of them were recognized.

Enigmatic Connections

Presumably, Klimt had great charisma, for he was neither tall nor classically good-looking. Photographs of him usually show him dressed in a ground-length painter's smock, beneath which he wore nothing but a pair of sandals. Almost all of his portraits are of females, mainly the wives and daughters of bankers, industrialists and members of the imperial court. His ability to make his sitters look extraordinarily glamorous must have enhanced his attraction. Klimt's studio was said to have been permanently populated with (often naked) reclining female models. At any moment, he would ask one or other of them to pose for him. Yet he did not limit himself to painting only beautiful young women, but depicted all forms of femininity, both symbolically

and physically, emphasizing aspects such as strength, childhood, pregnancy, old age and the loss of physical beauty.

Some historians have described Klimt as a sexual predator. Others have said he was an exploiter or hater of women, but his paintings suggest that he only had respect and admiration for them – even in

his depictions of old age. Certainly his paintings reveal no sense of misogyny, and no woman ever came forward to reproach him publicly. His work seems to imply that he viewed them ultimately as a phenomenon of nature. Overall he was a quiet man, devoted to his art, his family and small circle of friends, who avoided the fashionable Viennese café society. He once admitted that he was not entirely clear about his relationships when describing how, in 1899, he rushed home from Venice after a row about his advances towards 18-year-old Alma Schindler (1879–1964, later Alma Mahler, Gropius and, finally, Werfel). On his arrival in Vienna, his first action was to telegraph Emilie Flöge.

Emilie

Klimt and Emilie became close in the 1890s, soon after Ernst's death, and remained so for the rest of Klimt's life. They accompanied each other to the opera and took French lessons together. The intimacy between them is apparent in the nearly four hundred postcards and

letters that Klimt wrote to her between 1897 and 1917. Although none feature ardent declarations of love, they nevertheless express an intense intimacy between them and the comfort they drew from one another. At that time, the post was delivered more than once a day, and postcards were the fastest, most reliable method of conveying information. Klimt often sent Emilie several postcards in any one day, usually simply continuing earlier conversations, so they are full of trivial, disjointed information and are difficult to understand out of context. As final evidence of their closeness, when Klimt suffered a stroke in 1918, the first words he uttered were: 'Emilie soll kommen' ('Emilie come').

The Vienna Secession

After the deaths of his brother and father, Klimt's questioning of the conventions of academic painting gained momentum, not least because of the somewhat insulting way he was treated by the establishment. In 1893, he was told he was to be appointed professor at the Viennese Academy of Fine Arts, but, for some unexplained reason, the Ministry of Culture did not confirm this appointment. It suggested their lack of belief in his skills and he felt slighted. Added to his grief, he began focusing more on experimentation and the study of contemporary and ancient styles of art that were overlooked within traditional artistic circles, including Japanese, Chinese, ancient Egyptian and Mycenaean.

Modern Ideas

In recent years, Klimt had socialized with the most cultured circles of artists and patrons, and been exposed to a number of different influences. Vienna was attracting and nurturing numerous creative talents. Among several others living in the city at the time were the composers Gustav Mahler (1860–1911) and Brahms, the author and dramatist Arthur Schnitzler (1862–1931), the architects Otto Wagner (1841–1918) and Adolf Loos (1870–1933), and the 'Father of Psychoanalysis' Sigmund Freud (1836–1959). Klimt was also introduced to various creative ideas, including Symbolism, Art Nouveau (Jugendstil) and the Munich Secession. In response, by the end of 1896, he had become even more experimental with his painting style, particularly with his personal symbolism, even though he retained a certain loyalty towards traditional allegories and antiquity throughout his life.

The Vienna Künstlerhaus

In 1891, when Klimt was 29, the Künstlercompagnie had joined the Vienna Künstlerhaus, or the Viennese Co-operative Society of Austrian Artists. It was a powerful organization that encouraged academic art and helped to maintain standards and promote art in Vienna. It arranged commissions for its members and staged exhibitions. Yet many believed that it had too much of a monopoly on the city's art. The rumblings of artistic dissension across Vienna came to a head in April 1897, when Klimt and several other artists rebelled against the officialdom of the Vienna Künstlerhaus. Weary of the prejudices and restrictions implemented by the Künstlerhaus committee, numerous members resigned and set up a new, independent association: the Vereinigung Bildender Künstler Österreichs (also known as the Association of Austrian Artists or the Vienna Secession). This breakaway group had been inspired by the Munich Secession, a similar movement of young artists in Germany in 1892, who had defected from their local conservative art organization.

Independent Creative Decisions

The painters, sculptors and architects of the Vienna Secession elected Klimt as their first president. With no manifesto, they neither favoured nor encouraged any particular style of art or design, and they welcomed artists who worked in all styles, such as Naturalists, Symbolists and Realists. Their goals were to end the cultural isolation of Vienna, welcoming artists from abroad and making their work known in other countries; to provide independent art exhibitions without selection committees (or more open-minded ones); to make their own, independent creative decisions without having to adhere to strict expectations; and to publish a magazine showcasing their work.

Klimt and two of his close friends, the architect Josef Hoffmann (1870–1956) and the painter Carl Moll (1861–1945), were mainly responsible for the Secession exhibition programming from its inauguration until 1905. Somewhat surprisingly, the government supported them and gave

them a lease on public land to build an exhibition hall. With help from Hoffmann, another Secessionist, the architect Josef Maria Olbrich (1867–1908), designed their hall, and it became the Secessionists' landmark. Above its entrance a comment by the art critic Ludwig Hevesi (1843–1910) was emblazoned: 'Der Zeit ihre Kunst. Der Kunst ihre Freiheit' ('To every age its art. To art its liberty').

Ver Sacrum

From the first, the Secessionist exhibitions were popular with the public. Klimt designed and illustrated the poster for the first exhibition in 1898 (*see* page 37). His portrayal of *Theseus Fighting the Minotaur* was inspired by ancient Greek vases, and it inspired imitations, resulting in a new trend for a similarly sinuous, graphic style. Even the Emperor visited the inaugural exhibition, which displayed both the work of the Secessionists and that of many foreign artists, including Arnold Böcklin (1827–1901), Walter Crane (1845–1915), Alphonse Mucha (1860–1939), Edgar Degas (1834–1917), Pierre Puvis de Chavannes (1824–98), Fernand Khnopff (1858–1921) and Auguste Rodin (1840–1917).

Visitors were exposed to various new creative ideas, including changes in art that were occurring elsewhere in the art world. The Secessionists also chose a title for their magazine that suggested new life and hope: *Ver Sacrum*, or *Sacred Spring*. Initially published in 1898, Klimt contributed to the journal regularly for two years, although he preferred to show his feelings through paint rather than the written word. As they explored possibilities beyond the traditions of academic art, Secessionists aimed to herald in the new millennium with something completely new. With the support of the government, the new styles they developed were soon recognized as the Viennese version of Art Nouveau and, within a short time, the expression 'Sezessionstil,' or 'Secessionist style' was used to describe them.

Transition

In 1898, Klimt was given his first commission as a Secessionist. He was asked to decorate a room in the Ringstrasse mansion of Greek businessman Nikolaus Dumba (1830–1900). Years earlier, Makart had designed Dumba's study, and now Klimt was to design decorations for his music room. Along with a mural, Klimt produced two paintings: *Music II* and *Schubert at the Piano*. As with all his work, he had prepared for the two paintings with hundreds of sketches and everything was meticulously researched and planned, from the compositions, to his palette, to the order and method of paint application, and where the light would fall on the works in the room.

The overall appearance of the paintings revealed a new, soft, almost Impressionistic style, with a delicate, warm, golden light appearing to emanate from the candlelight that illuminated the figures. The paintings were admired by all who saw them, both for their style and their subjects. Franz Schubert (1797–1828) was a national hero and, in general, music was perceived in contemporary Viennese society to

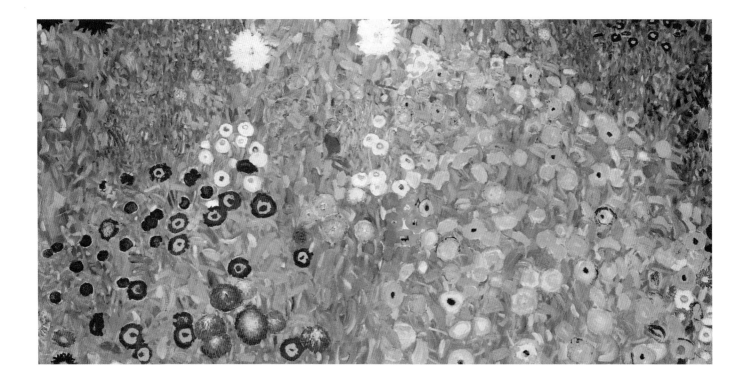

be a sign of a secure and well-ordered life. The image of Schubert was a good likeness, but Klimt's point was that he was now focusing more on symbolism and the creation of mood.

Sonja Knips

During the same year that Klimt worked on Dumba's music room, he was commissioned to paint a portrait of Sonja Knips (*see* page 99), née Baroness Poitiers des Eschelles, for her new mansion, designed and built by Hoffmann on the occasion of her marriage. Klimt painted several other works for the house as well. In the portrait, Knips wears an elaborate, gauzy, pale pink dress with a high, ruffled neck. Her left arm grips her chair as she leans forward. Klimt and she had known each other for several years, long before she married her wealthy husband, and there was even a suggestion that there had been a romance between them that Klimt did not pursue. A highly intelligent woman, she was extremely supportive of the Vienna Secession and the idea of a new Viennese art. In his portrait of her, Klimt dispensed with the hard outlines of academic paintings, instead allowing the young woman's dress to fade gently into the untraditionally empty background. This new, softer style was an indication that, at last, Klimt was moving away from the powerful influence of Makart.

Pallas Athene

Klimt showed seven works in the second Secession exhibition of 1898, including his portrayal of the Secessionists' symbol, the Greek goddess of just causes, wisdom and the arts, *Pallas Athene* (*see* page 42). On a square canvas, his version of her was not of a traditional, glowing goddess, but of a modern, fiery and formidable auburn-haired woman. Wearing an imposing helmet covering her face, she regards viewers with an appraising look. On her golden coin breastplate is the face of Medusa, the tongue protruding. Standing on the orb in her right hand is a nude figure, possibly symbolizing the frailty of the human race. With a liberal application of gold leaf and a decorative frame made by Klimt's goldsmith brother Georg to his specifications, the painting demonstrated a new move towards opulent embellishment and a blatant embrace of the Art Nouveau preference for ornamentation. Yet it was also unlike anything else that others were producing at the time,

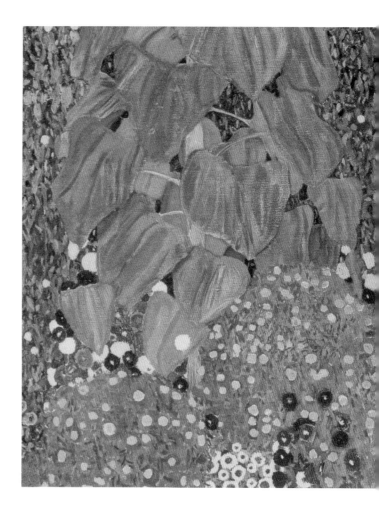

an amalgamation of several styles and influences, but still Klimt's purely personal interpretation.

Femmes Fatales

One of Klimt's favourite themes appeared to be strong women, something that developed particularly during his Secessionist period. With her armour and weapons, *Pallas Athene* was the first of these, and others followed. The female form was an important element in Art Nouveau, but Klimt portrayed his women as being particularly strong, provocative and often almost formidable during an era when women were expected to be compliant and demure. In 1898, as a line drawing in the first edition of *Ver Sacrum*, he portrayed *Nuda Veritas*, or *Naked Truth*; a nude femme fatale, boldly looking out from the

Loosely translated, this reads: 'If you cannot please everyone by your deeds and your art, just please a few. To attempt to please everyone is dangerous.' The painting scandalized bourgeois Viennese viewers, mainly because it shows pubic hair. The woman makes no attempt to hide her nudity, nor to cast down her eyes decorously. Her pale complexion, abundant auburn hair and bold stare give the impression of audacity and a lack of feminine propriety. In holding the mirror up to viewers, she asks us to see ourselves as we really are. Her stance and gaze were unacceptable at a time when the public was accustomed to idealized, demure nudes and, consequently, the work was reviled.

The Faculty Paintings

In 1894, Klimt and Matsch had received a commission from the Ministry of Education to make a number of ceiling paintings for the Great Hall of the University of Vienna, depicting the various faculties in allegorical form. The overall theme was to be the victory of intellect over ignorance, glorifying learning and knowledge and its usefulness to society. Klimt was assigned the subjects of philosophy, medicine and jurisprudence, while Matsch was responsible for theology and the ceiling's central painting: *The Triumph of Light over Darkness.*

From the start of the undertaking, the two artists disagreed over what to include in their paintings and their style. By then, Klimt was moving away from a strict adherence to academic art, while Matsch was conforming to it as closely as ever. As they could not agree, the paintings remained unfinished for many years and, even by 1900, Klimt's work for *Philosophy* was not fully complete. However, he decided to show his work in progress that year to members of the university. After the success of his previous public paintings, anticipation was high, but, when the painting was revealed, onlookers were confused and angered.

Philosophy

Philosophy demonstrated Klimt's evolution to a bolder, more ornate style, and his retreat into his own symbolic expression. Critics were disturbed by the content of the work: a column of naked men and women apparently drifting aimlessly. At the bottom of the long

page. The following year, he painted a two-metre high version of her (*see* page 43). The red-headed nude woman holds up the mirror of truth, while the snake of falsehood lies dead at her feet.

Surrounded by a painted gold frame, the work also features, in elaborately stylized lettering, a quotation by the German dramatist Friedrich Schiller (1759–1805):

> *Kannst du nicht allen gefallen durch deine Tat*
> *und dein Kunstwerk, mach es wenigen recht. Vielen*
> *gefallen ist schlimm.*

canvas, a female head stares out. In the exhibition catalogue, she was described as 'Knowledge', but viewers did not understand what it all meant. Members of the university, the clergy and art critics were dismayed. The clergy was offended by the blatant nudity, and academics and critics were upset by Klimt's apparent challenging of convention, lack of glorification of scientific achievements and inexplicable symbolism.

Klimt's figures represented human existence and the continuous emergence of life from the universal void; he intended them to depict how minds and intelligence take human form. Nevertheless, within days of the work being exhibited in Vienna, 87 members of the university protested about it. Despite the outcry it provoked in Vienna, when Klimt sent *Philosophy* to the 1900 Exposition Universelle in Paris, it was awarded a Gold Medal. Meanwhile, in Austria, the controversy continued.

Medicine

Although affected by the contention, Klimt exhibited his unfinished second painting *Medicine* (*see* page 45), a year after he had shown *Philosophy*, and then continued to work on it. Also featuring a column of figures, *Medicine* once again represents humanity as a floating column of bodies, this time mainly female, at various stages of life. It includes a character from Greek myths, Hygieia, the goddess of health and the daughter of Aesculapius, the first doctor. The work exacerbated the scandal. Within the line of figures, the presence of Death seemed to mock all that doctors were trying to do. Philosophers had been horrified by *Philosophy*; now physicians were furious about *Medicine*. Many found the image depressing and disconcerting, and the nudity and symbolism pornographic and unnecessary, but, most of all, the painting did not seem to celebrate the advances in medicine that had been made in recent years.

Jurisprudence

In the midst of this row, and following his disappointment at not having been appointed professor at the Academy of Fine Arts in 1893, Klimt reapplied for the position. Perhaps not surprisingly in the

light of the current scandal, he was not given the post. It was the last time he applied to teach anywhere.

In 1903, he exhibited *Jurisprudence*, his final painting for the university alongside *Philosophy* and *Medicine*. Although the symbolism in the new work was similar to the previous two, the painting style had changed. *Jurisprudence* was bolder, flatter and brighter. To contemporary eyes, it was just as shocking, however, and it was condemned as vehemently as the previous two paintings. It featured three female figures, representing Truth, Justice and Law, looking down on four gaunt, naked figures – the Three Furies and a man who is bound and held by an octopus. Perceived as representing revenge rather than justice, the painting caused public outcry.

Withdrawal and Separation

Controversial for their perceived indecency, lack of optimism and departure from Klimt's original plans, the Faculty Paintings were a problem for the authorities. Eventually, the Ministry for Education decided to put them in a museum rather than in the university. When it was also decided not to send them to the 1904 World Fair in St Louis, the usually reserved Klimt was angered. Announcing that he was withdrawing from the commission, he refused to hand the paintings over and repaid the amount that he had already received for them. They were eventually destroyed in 1945 by retreating German forces.

The conflict over the university paintings led to the final separation between Klimt and Matsch. Their styles had been diversifying when they began the project and, by 1903 it was apparent that Klimt's leanings towards the radical new ideas of Art Nouveau, with dynamic curves and an emphasis on nature and decoration, contrasted directly with the conventional work produced by Matsch. Within a few months, Matsch moved out of their joint studio and Klimt never again pursued a public assignment.

The Golden Phase

More than one Secessionist exhibition was held each year and, in 1902, the fourteenth exhibition was held with a special theme to celebrate the composer Ludwig van Beethoven (1770–1827). The interior of the building was completely refurbished for the event. Numerous sculptures and paintings created an appropriate setting for the centrepiece of the exhibition: a monumental marble and bronze statue of Beethoven by the German sculptor Max Klinger (1857–1920). For three of the exhibition entrance walls, Klimt created a seven-part frieze.

The Beethoven Frieze

Heavily embellished with gold and silver leaf, fragments of semi-precious materials, and other odds and ends including nails, buttons, tin tacks and pieces of mirror and coloured glass, Klimt's huge *Beethoven Frieze* (1902, *see* pages 47–51) created a powerful impact, although the complex work has not always been understood. It refers to the final chorus of Beethoven's 'Ninth Symphony', which was performed at the opening of the exhibition by the Vienna Opera Chorus. Klimt also used symbolism to suggest the salvation of the human race through art and love, and although not everyone could work out its meaning, the ambitious work was admired immediately for its lyrical and ornate style. The frieze does not correspond directly to Beethoven's score, but it is Klimt's personal interpretation of the music, as well as his continuing exploration into the meaning of human existence, which he had started exploring in his Faculty Paintings. The frieze also represented an allegory of cultural forces, the role of art and of the artist as saviour, a vision shared by the other Secessionists.

When the frieze was exhibited in 1902, Klimt had already shown both *Philosophy* and *Medicine*, but had not yet completed *Jurisprudence*. For the first time in his career, he was facing hostile criticism, yet the *Beethoven Frieze* gained wide acclaim. Even Rodin congratulated him on his 'so tragic and so divine' work. Rodin had been exhibiting in Vienna since 1882, including at the first Secessionist exhibition in 1898, and the two artists admired each other's work. Klimt had featured two figures from Rodin's sculpture *The Gates of Hell* in *Philosophy*. In 1905, he also borrowed elements from Rodin's *Celle qui fut la Belle Heaulmière* of *c.* 1885–87 in *The Three Ages of Woman* (*see* page 56).

It was originally planned that the *Beethoven Frieze* would be removed after the exhibition, so Klimt painted on the cheapest materials he could: a plastered wooden lattice, held in place with reeds. Ultimately, the work proved to be so admired that it remained there long after the exhibition had ended, and was later saved by a collector. It had deteriorated quite rapidly, but has since been restored and it is often considered to have been the turning point in Klimt's career.

Square Landscapes

While spending several summers with Emilie and other members of her family, at the Flöge country house on Lake Attersee in the Salzkammergut area of Austria, Klimt began to paint landscapes on square canvases that became an important feature of his work (*see* pages 66–93). He believed that the square shape created a sense of tranquillity, emulating the totality of the universe. His landscapes were unlike any other painted at the time. They did not explore skies or light or atmospheric views. Instead, they resembled richly embellished or embroidered textiles, combining strong colour, interesting shapes and flowing rhythms.

A Gilded Touch

Although he rarely travelled beyond Austria, in 1899, Klimt visited Venice, where he studied its gilded, mosaic-like art, Murano glass and the ornate architecture. In 1902, he travelled to Ravenna, where he studied the Byzantine mosaics for which the city is famous. He even exhibited at the Biennale di Venezia in 1910. The glittering and colourful art he had seen profoundly affected him. He felt an affinity with it and with his own concept of decorated images and, once he was back in Vienna, his frequent use of gold and silver leaf recalled the art he had so admired in Italy. As always, he also drew on a blend of wider influences, including abstraction, Mycenaean ornamentation and elements he had been featuring in his landscape paintings.

Embellished Women

Klimt's portraits of women of the time began blending sensuality with the coolness of Oriental motifs, particularly inspired by the Japanese 'pillar prints' he collected. His deliberate contrasts between finely modelled, delicately coloured faces and hands, and two-dimensional, elaborately patterned golden surfaces enhanced his portrayal of his sitters' characters. Their flat, decorated clothing and backgrounds are as important as their lifelike faces. Subtly, the embellishments serve to

unveil each woman's personality, surrounding and highlighting her realistic face, neck and hands. The period became known as Klimt's 'Golden Phase'. Although he had used gold in some previous paintings, such as *Pallas Athene* of 1898, *Judith I* of 1901 (*see* page 44) and *Goldfish* of 1901–02 (*see* page 46), and his *Beethoven Frieze* of 1902, he soon began to feature especially sumptuous ornamentation on a

regular basis in paintings such as the *Portrait of Adele Bloch-Bauer I* (1907, *see* page 61) and *The Kiss* (1907, *see* page 62). His ideas were still often controversial, but, in the main, the period was marked by positive critical reaction and subsequent financial success. His 'Golden Phase' reached its peak in 1907.

New Departures

In May 1903, Josef Hoffmann and the painter and designer Koloman Moser (1868–1918) set up the Wiener Werkstätte, or the Vienna Workshop. Evolving from the Vienna Secession, it was a co-operative for artist workers, modelled on the English Arts and Crafts movement, following the ideas of William Morris (1834–96) and John Ruskin (1819–1900), the Guild of Handicraft set up by Charles Robert Ashbee (1863–1942), and the elegant style of the architect and designer Charles Rennie Mackintosh (1868–1928), although it made greater use of technology.

Established to sell members' practical designs and also to train young, promising designers in specialist techniques, ultimately the goals of the Werkstätte were to address the problems that had affected crafts as the result of industrialization. Werkstätte members adhered to the Arts and Crafts theories of objects being created by specialist artists, architects and designers using time, care and pride to counteract the burgeoning fashion for cheap, mass-produced goods.

Klimt and the Werkstätte

Hoffmann and Moser found premises for the Werkstätte and, by 1905, they had about one hundred employees. By 1907, they had also created their own café and cabaret, the Cabaret Fledermaus. As a member of its board of management, Klimt was closely involved and often collaborated with the Werkstätte, painting pictures for interiors or designing fabrics and furniture. In 1904, he worked with them on fitting out the interior of the Flöge fashion house in Vienna, which was owned by the three Flöge sisters Helene, Emilie and Pauline. As well as the stylish interiors, the sisters welcomed Klimt's and Moser's fabric and dress designs that featured, unusually for the time, strong contrasts and vibrant colours and patterns.

Dress Design

Along with the women's rights movement that was spreading across Europe, the reform dress developed as an anti-fashion movement, liberating women from restrictive clothing such as corsets. Making dresses was part of the Secessionist principle of blurring boundaries between art and craft, and the designs that Klimt created for the Flöge fashion house were also a statement against the rigidity of Viennese society. In 1906, he photographed Emilie wearing some of the reform dresses they had both designed. As with his Lake Attersee landscape paintings, his textile patterns also had a direct influence on his painting style of the time.

A Retrospective

In 1903, the year that *Ver Sacrum* ceased publication, the eighteenth Secessionist Exhibition was devoted entirely to Klimt and, for the first time, he showed some of his landscapes, such as *Fruit Trees* and *Beech Grove I* (*see* page 73). The style and significance of these corresponded with his developing ideas about embellishment, colour and mood. In the same show, he exhibited some portraits of women, including *Emilie Flöge* (*see* page 52) and *Gertha Felsövanyi* (both 1902). They were the first of his new trademark style, featuring a single woman wearing an elaborate outfit rendered two-dimensionally, set against a plain background and heightened with gold. Only their hands and faces are painted realistically. At a time when the new ideas of the Secession were losing momentum with the public, and Klimt's allegorical work was still often misunderstood, these portraits of society women remained popular and continued to be commissioned.

The Stoclet Palace

In 1904, Hoffmann received a commission to build a mansion in Brussels for a young Belgian industrialist, Adolphe Stoclet (1871–1949). Between 1905 and 1911, Hoffmann and the Wiener Werkstätte built the Stoclet Palace. It became one of the grandest monuments of the Art Nouveau era. Klimt decorated three walls of the dining room with a mosaic frieze consisting of nine panels. Using expensive materials, including enamel, glass, ceramics, metals, coral, mother-of-pearl and semi-precious jewels, his *Stoclet Frieze* (*see* pages 57–60)

offset the clean lines of Hoffmann's building and furniture, while the ornate panels, including *The Tree of Life*, *Expectation* and *Fulfilment* feature symbolic motifs. He had learned the technique of mosaic at the Kunstgewerbeschule and had been further inspired by the mosaics of Ravenna, but he also considered Stoclet's interest in Indian and

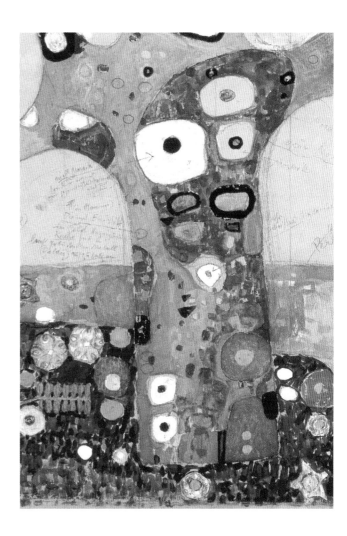

Buddhist art and, as always, researched the work intensely before completing it. His resulting exotic designs included elements of Asian and Byzantine art. With triangular leaves and circular flowers, *The Tree of Life* is the frieze's main motif, suggesting sacred myths, religions and philosophies of various cultures. The *Stoclet Frieze* was the last of Klimt's mural works.

Break with the Secession

Meanwhile, discord within the Secession movement reached a crisis. In 1905, an established conflict between the artists who painted in a naturalist style – known as 'the naturalists' – and the more versatile artists – known as 'the stylists' – finally erupted. The naturalists resented the success of the stylists and believed that they were dominating the Viennese art market; the stylists believed that the naturalists were not adhering to the fundamental beliefs of the Secession, that is, to create more original, independent art. Declaring that they could no longer be associated with those artists who refused to embrace their principles, Klimt and a large faction (the so-called

'stylists'), including Moll, Hoffmann, Moser and Wagner, left the Secession. The event caused a sensation in Vienna.

Later Style

The breakaway artists and architects, who were at first called the 'Klimt Group', had nowhere to exhibit. Then, in 1908, when they expressed a wish to put on an exhibition to commemorate the sixtieth anniversary of Emperor Franz Joseph's accession to the throne, the government lent them some land for a temporary venue. Hoffmann built them a pavilion and they began calling their new association 'Kunstschau', or Art Show.

The Kiss

As well as portraits and landscapes, at the 1908 Kunstschau, Klimt exhibited several allegories, including *The Kiss*. Painted the previous year, the work represents the culmination of his Golden Phase. In its subject matter, use of gold and silver leaf, brilliant colours, symbolism and sinuous curves of Art Nouveau, it is often considered one of the most important works of the Viennese Jugendstil and Klimt's most famous work. *The Kiss* features a man and woman in an embrace. Klimt had included similar embraces in the *Beethoven* and *Stoclet* friezes, but *The Kiss* broke new ground. For once, Klimt's representation of a female figure is submissive. The couple are on their knees and the man leans over the woman to kiss her tenderly. Emotion is expressed through their body language, particularly the positions of their hands and the woman's facial expression. They represent the mystical union of spiritual and erotic love, and the connection of life and the universe. Feminine energy is displayed through flowing lines on the woman's clothing in swirling, colourful floral motifs, while masculine energy on the man's clothing is represented by black and silver straight lines and rectangles.

Allegory and Influence

Besides *The Kiss*, Klimt showed two other allegories at the 1908 Kunstschau. They were *Hope II* (*see* page 63) and *Danaë* (*see* page 64). *Hope II* shows a pregnant woman in an embellished dress, standing with her head bent, a group of worshipping women kneeling at her feet. The work resembles a religious icon. *Danaë* blatantly represents the ecstasy of love. Next to her naked, coiled figure is a torrent of golden coins, the golden rain of Zeus. These and other allegorical paintings of the time show Klimt's fascination with life and death, partly a result of his periods of depression and partly generated by the turbulent atmosphere in Europe leading up to the First World War. At the time, a new generation of artists was also working in Vienna, and, just as Klimt had idolized Makart, several of these younger artists revered him. Among them were Egon Schiele (1890–1918) and Oskar Kokoschka (1886–1980), who had moved completely away from the academic art that Klimt had felt obliged to adhere to at the start of his career.

While the 1908 Kunstschau had exhibited only contemporary Austrian art, architecture and design, in 1909, the group held a second and final exhibition. This time, they also invited international artists to join them. Klimt showed 16 new paintings, while artists from beyond the group whose work was represented included Schiele, Kokoschka, Munch, Pierre Bonnard (1867–1947), Edouard Vuillard (1868–1940), Jan Toorop (1858–1928), Henri Matisse (1869–1954), Paul Gauguin (1848–1903) and Vincent van Gogh (1853–90). Due to a lack of financial success, however, no further shows on this scale were organized by the group. Nonetheless, it had served to inspire Klimt. The range of expression he had seen in works by the other European artists had overwhelmed him and, later that year, he travelled to Paris and Madrid with Carl Moll. In the latter, he was particularly fascinated by the work of El Greco (1541–1614) and in Paris by the work of Henri de Toulouse-Lautrec (1864–1901) and by Fauvism – the brightly coloured, distorted paintings being produced by artists including Matisse and André Derain (1880–1954).

Subsequently, Klimt reconsidered his own golden style and decided that it was inferior by comparison. He realized that the gold and embellishment was actually restraining him and preventing greater exploration of psychology and symbolism. From the moment he returned to Vienna, his work began to show the influence of several other younger artists, including Kokoschka, van Gogh and Toulouse-Lautrec. For instance, two of the first paintings he executed, *Lady with Hat and Feather Boa* (1909, *see* page 108) and *The Black*

Feather Hat (1910, *see* page 109) reflect a strong influence of Toulouse-Lautrec and, to a lesser extent, Kokoschka. The style was a marked departure from his previous portraits of society ladies.

Fauvist Phase

Although Klimt painted the same subjects as he always had – that is, portraits, landscapes and allegories – from 1910, he developed his new style, demonstrating greater expression, a freer technique and a colourful yet still ornamented style. His paintings continued to be vibrant and powerful, but with a marked absence of gold and other decorative embellishments. One of his last pictures in his golden style was *Death and Life* of 1910 (*see* page 110), which was shown at the

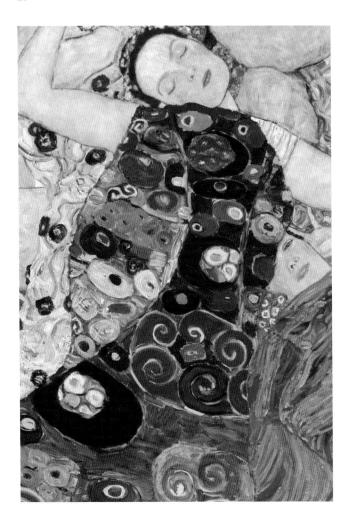

1911 Esposizione Internazionale d'Arte in Rome and won first place. In 1915, however, he reworked the painting, including changing the background from gold to blue. His new, more expressive works can be seen to have built on several influences. For instance, his fluid *Portrait of Mäda Primavesi* of 1912 (*see* page 113), his only major portrait of a child, draws on ideas from a number of sources, including Schiele, Kokoschka, Matisse and Japanese woodcuts.

Final Years

Klimt rarely wrote about his paintings or his methods, but once, in a rare commentary, he stated: 'I have never painted a self-portrait. I am less interested in myself as a subject for a painting than I am in other people, above all, women…. There is nothing special about me. I am a painter who paints day after day from morning to night…. Whoever wants to know something about me … ought to look carefully at my pictures.'

Changing Styles

Although his style changed over the course of his career, Klimt always painted and drew what gave him pleasure, fusing symbolism with historicism, pattern, colour and an academic style, all augmented by the influence of an eclectic range of other sources. He lived during the last years of the Habsburg Empire and through the horrors of the First World War, but his work reflects none of the social and political upheavals that occurred around him. In his allegories, portraits and landscapes, Klimt portrayed a sense of luxury and sensuousness that had not been seen since the Rococo era of the late eighteenth century, and the importance he placed on ornament never diminished, even when, in later years, he began using a broader palette and looser, more confident brushwork.

To understand some of Klimt's stylistic changes, many of his recurring themes and subjects can be compared, such as *Hope I* of 1903 and *Hope II* of 1907–08 (*see* pages 53 and 63), or his portraits, *Adele Bloch-Bauer I* of 1907 and *Adele Bloch-Bauer II* of 1912 (*see* pages 61 and 114). His decorative art typified the spirit of the Ringstrasse era and came to represent European Art Nouveau. At times, his portrayals of taboo subjects attracted fierce criticism and scandalized society, while, at other times, he was the darling of the art world. Klimt's portraits of aristocratic and wealthy women, however, never lost favour and they brought him financial security, respect and renown, and generally, during the last decade of his life, his work was more popular than ever.

The Forest Demon

Klimt's trip to Madrid and Paris in 1909 was the last time he left Austria. Although he represented his country at the 1910 Venice Biennale, he did not travel there. After 1912, he began taking an annual cure at the spa at Bad Gastein in the Austrian state of Salzburg, although there is no evidence that he was suffering from any illness. In the last few years of his life, he spent much of his time in his studio and garden in Heitzing, and at the Flöge family home on Lake Attersee. Klimt's landscape paintings were affected by his later stylistic changes, but they remained lavishly ornamental, with emphatic patterning and rich colouring. The locals nicknamed him 'Waldschrat' ('forest demon') because he spent so much time painting in the open air in Attersee – a contrast with his usual studio practice in Vienna. Because of the flattening effects he created in his landscapes, it is thought that he used a telescope to paint several of them. In 1915, Klimt's mother, Anna, died, prompting his depression, and he began using a toned-down palette.

Klimt's Patrons

Despite controversies over some of his work, there were enough wealthy individuals in Vienna anxious to buy or commission work from Klimt, and there was usually a waiting list for his portraits. As he produced only one portrait a year, his patrons were not numerous, but, by 1914, he could demand extremely high prices for his work. Klimt's patrons were nearly all men who had made their fortune in commerce during the Ringstrasse era. Several also commissioned Hoffmann to design villas and mansions for them, and most of their wives patronized the Wiener Werkstätte for clothes, jewellery and furniture. Almost all were Jewish and, apart from Stoclet, either Austrian or Hungarian. Their names include Knips, Bloch, Wittgenstein, Primavesi, Henneberg, Gallia and Lederer.

Legacy

On 28 June 1914 at Sarajevo in Serbia, Emperor Franz Joseph's heir, the Archduke Franz-Ferdinand, was assassinated with his wife, Sophie, by a South Slav nationalist. One month later, Austria-Hungary declared war on Serbia, triggering the First World War. At the end of the war, after appalling suffering and a massive death toll, Austria-Hungary ceased to exist and the entire world had changed.

On 11 January 1918, exactly 10 months before the First World War ended, Klimt suffered a stroke, leaving him paralyzed on his right side. He asked for Emilie to come to his bedside, and 26 days later, on 6 February, he died from pneumonia and influenza. He was 55. By the time of his death, his optimistic, extravagant art had become outdated.

Movements such as Cubism, Futurism, Dada and Constructivism had been established, but Klimt's legacy continued nonetheless. Although he left no school of painting, his work was crucial in the evolution of art from the nineteenth century to the twentieth, and his influence on illustration was momentous. Throughout the second half of the twentieth century, his work became particularly appreciated and, by the early twenty-first century, his paintings, drawings and prints commanded some of the highest prices ever recorded for individual works of art.

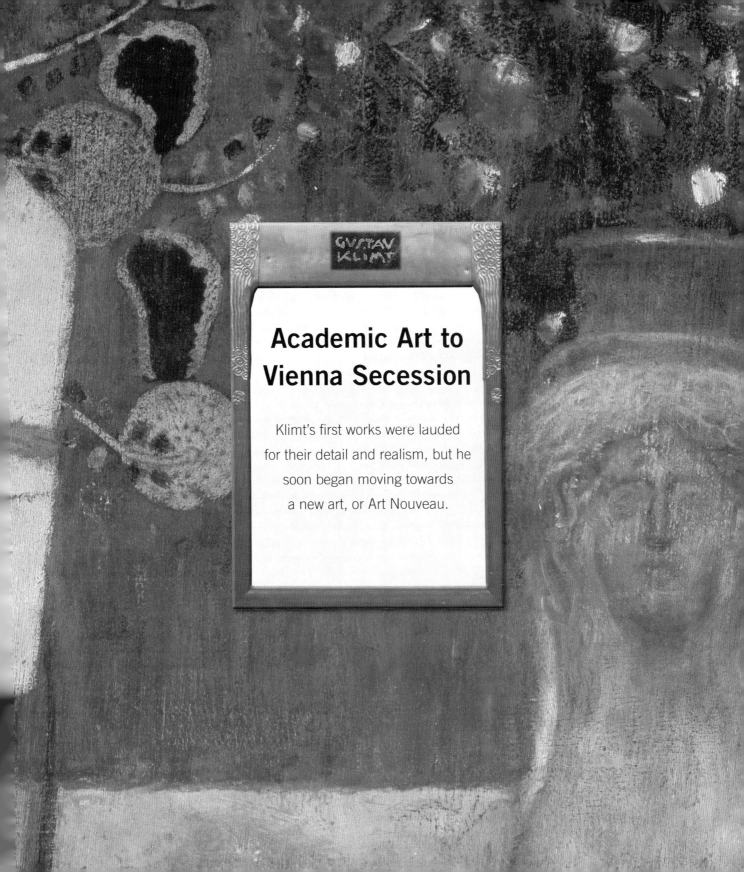

GVSTAV KLIMT

Academic Art to Vienna Secession

Klimt's first works were lauded
for their detail and realism, but he
soon began moving towards
a new art, or Art Nouveau.

Fable, 1883
Oil on canvas, 84.5 x 117 cm (33 x 46 in)
• Kunsthistorisches Museum, Vienna

Painted when he was 21 and had just completed his studies, Klimt's work from an early age focused on the beauty of the female form. This was for the set of books *Allegories and Emblems*.

Idyll, 1884
Oil on canvas, 49.5 x 73.5 cm (19½ x 29 in)
• Kunsthistorisches Museum, Vienna

An illustration for one of the three volumes called *Allegories and Emblems* that Klimt worked on early in his career, this classically inspired painting also took elements from Renaissance works, particularly Michelangelo and Raphael's compositions and figures.

The Theatre in Taormina, 1886–88
Oil on canvas, 240 x 400 cm (94½ x 157½ in)
• Burgtheater, Vienna

Commissioned to continue Makart's work after his untimely death, Klimt painted this on the stairway of the Kunsthistorisches Museum. The work displays Klimt's love of lavish design and the classical art of ancient Greece.

Auditorium in the Old Burgtheater, Vienna, 1888
Gouache on paper, 82 x 92 cm (36 x 32 in)
• Kunsthistorisches Museum, Vienna

When the Old Burgtheater closed for the last time in 1888, Klimt took the opportunity to show his portraiture skills, capturing the likenesses of nearly two hundred society figures and casting the audience as players.

Allegory of Love, 1895
Oil on canvas, 60 x 44 cm (23 x 17 in)
• Kunsthistorisches Museum, Vienna

Painted in an academic style, this was one of Klimt's first portrayals of a romantic embrace. It reflects the late-nineteenth-century opinion that women should be aloof and passive when being wooed.

Music I, 1895
Oil on canvas, 37 x 44.5 cm (14½ x 17½ in)
• Neue Pinakothek, Munich

In 1898, when Klimt was commissioned to decorate Nikolaus Dumba's music room, he based his painting *Music II* on this, an example of his admiration of classical Greek imagery and his early use of gold leaf.

Tragedy, 1897
Black chalk and pen with gold, 42 x 31 cm (16½ x 12 in)
• Kunsthistorisches Museum, Vienna

The illustrations Klimt produced for the set of books *Allegories and Emblems* were intended to provide a guide to all the themes that had been used throughout the history of art. Aubrey Beardsley's influence is apparent.

Poster for the first Vienna Secession exhibition, 1898
Lithograph, 97 x 70 cm (38 x 27½ in) • Private Collection

Trying to establish a more modern style of art in Vienna, the Secessionists used Klimt's *Theseus Fighting the Minotaur* as the poster for their first exhibition and the cover of their new magazine, *Ver Sacrum*.

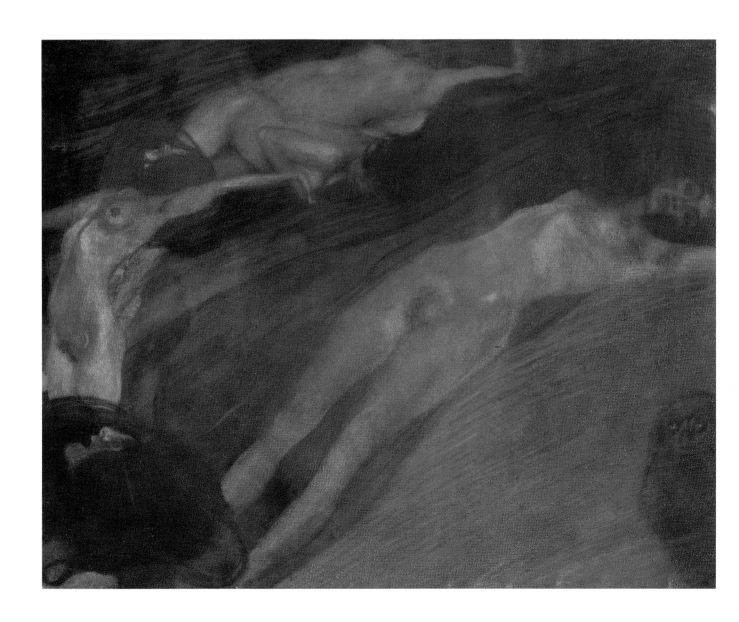

Moving Water, 1898
Oil on canvas, 52 x 65 cm (20½ x 25½ in)
• New York, Galerie St. Etienne; Private Collection

Demonstrating the flowing, sensuous lines of Art Nouveau, this softly painted image horrified many, as the women display their nudity with abandon. Klimt followed this with a similar image as an engraving in *Ver Sacrum*.

Water Nymphs (Silver Fish), *c.* **1899**
Oil on canvas, 82 x 52 cm (20½ x 21¾ in) • Private Collection

One of Klimt's strangest images, these two heads and long, flowing black hair seem to depict water nymphs of mythology, and yet they have no bodies. With tadpole-like silhouettes, their facial features are of modern women.

The Golden Phase

The paintings Klimt produced
from approximately 1899
to 1910, often using gold
leaf and other embellishments,
were some of his most
admired – or shocking.

Pallas Athene or Minerva, 1898
Oil and gold on canvas, 75 x 75 cm (29½ x 29½ in)
• Kunsthistorisches Museum, Vienna

'… Her terrible eyes shining …' is a quotation from *The Iliad* about the Greek goddess Pallas Athene. Klimt's depiction of her exudes formidable, divine power and was one of his first works to incorporate gold leaf.

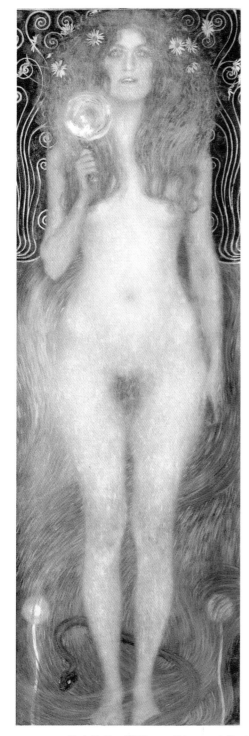

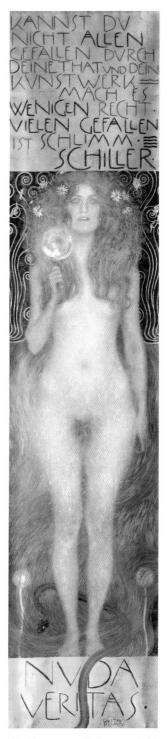

Nuda Veritas, 1899
Oil and gold on canvas, 25.2 x 55.2 cm (100 x 22 in)
• Austrian National Library, Vienna

This sensual, life-size nude stands in swirling blue waves, while the serpent at her feet suggests the biblical Eve. A soft, Impressionist-inspired technique and the figure's delicate, daisy-strewn hair contrast with her audacious, forthright gaze.

Judith with the Head of Holofernes, 1901
Oil on canvas, frame of embossed copper made by Georg Klimt,
84 x 42 cm (60¼ x 52 in) • Kunsthistorisches Museum, Vienna

Evoking Byzantine or Russian icons, this is Klimt's interpretation of a (modern) Judith holding the severed head of Holofernes, Nebuchadnezzar's general, who was threatening Judith's town. With her opulent jewels, Judith's beauty aligns with her power.

Hygieia (detail of Medicine), 1900–07
Oil on canvas, 300 x 430 cm (118 x 169¼ in)
• Destroyed by fire in 1945

Medicine featured a column of nude figures representing the river of life. Beneath them, Hygieia, goddess of health and medicine, stood like a femme fatale. Critics complained that Klimt was showing medicine to be helpless before mortality. Destroyed by fire in 1945.

Goldfish, 1901–02
Oil on canvas, 181 x 66.5 cm (71¼ x 26 in)
• Swiss Institute for Art Research, Zurich

Subtitled 'To My Critics', this was Klimt's response to complaints that his Faculty Paintings were too erotic for public display. The naked young woman at the bottom of the canvas turns her posterior to the audience and laughs.

The Beethoven Frieze (detail: Knight in Shining Armour), 1902
Casein paint, stucco, gold and graphite,
215 x 341 cm (84½ x 134¼ in) • Secession Building, Vienna

These skeletal figures of suffering in the Secession Building in Vienna represent the longing of all humans for true happiness. They plead with a knight in shining armour to obtain happiness for them, but first he will have to fight those in the following picture.

The Beethoven Frieze (detail: The Longing for Happiness Finds Repose in Poetry), 1902 • Casein paint, stucco, gold and graphite, 215 x 341 cm (84½ x 134¼ in) • Secession Building, Vienna

This section of the *Beethoven Frieze* in the Secession Building in Vienna depicts 'The Forces of Evil,' including 'Disease, Madness, Death, Desire and Lewdness, Licentiousness and Nagging Grief'. Klimt's academic style has been eradicated.

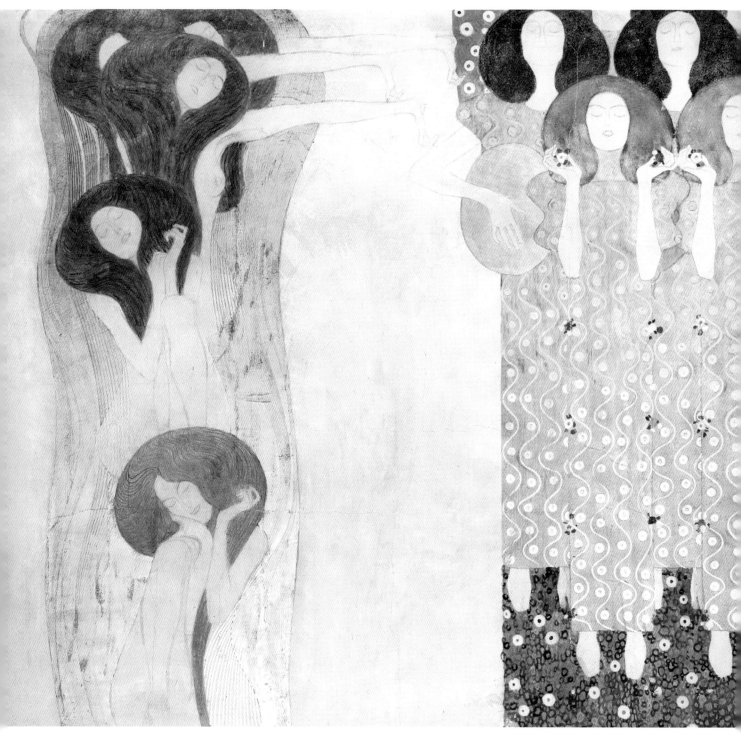

The Beethoven Frieze (detail: The Arts, Chorus of Paradise, Embrace), 1902 • Casein paint, stucco, gold and graphite, 215 x 341 cm (84½ x 134¼ in) • Secession Building, Vienna

This section of Klimt's *Beethoven Frieze* in the Secession Building in Vienna illustrates how all humans desire happiness, but, in an unpredictable world, the only guarantee of comfort and fulfilment can come from the arts, such as Beethoven's 'Ode to Joy'.

Emilie Flöge, 1902
Oil on canvas, 181 x 84 cm (71¼ x 33 in)
• Kunsthistorisches Museum, Vienna

Klimt and Emilie Flöge were particularly close for over twenty years, but there is no evidence that they were lovers. Klimt designed fabrics and loose-fitting, informal dresses such as this for Emilie and her fashion house.

Hope I, 1903
Oil on canvas, 181 x 67 cm (74½ x 26 in)
• National Gallery of Canada, Ottawa

Allegories of life and death were recurring themes for Klimt. The pregnant woman's nakedness was considered offensive by contemporary critics, so Klimt had a frame made with doors to cover the image.

The Golden Knight, or Life is a Struggle, 1903
Oil on canvas, 100 x 100 cm (39 x 39 in) • Private Collection.

Klimt used the icon of a knight in shining armour several times to represent hope, purity and chivalry. He was optimistic that these virtues would become more prevalent in Viennese society if he painted them.

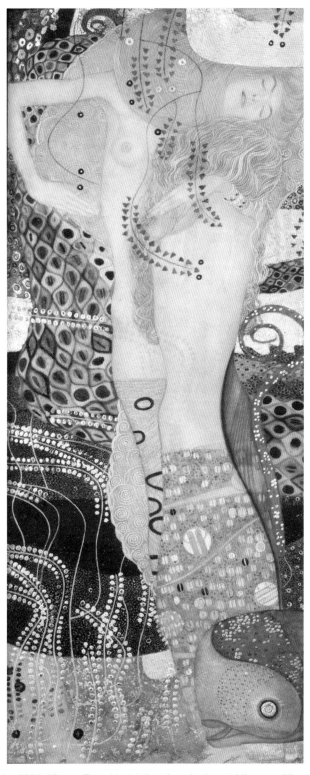

Water Serpents I, or The Hydra, 1904–07
Tempera, watercolour and gold on parchment, 50 × 20 cm (19¾ × 7 in)
• Österreichische Galerie Belvedere, Vienna

The gold paint, threads and patterns twisting around the women's bodies, and the allegorical title of this work, made it acceptable to the Viennese, even though it portrays two naked lesbians embracing each other.

The Three Ages of Woman, 1905
Oil, silver and gold on canvas, 178 x 198 cm (70 x 78 in)
• Galleria Nazionale d'Arte Moderna, Rome

Awarded the gold medal at the Esposizione Internazionale d'Arte in Rome in 1911, this work illustrates the passing of time. A elderly naked woman weeps and a young mother embraces her sleeping baby daughter.

The Stoclet Frieze: Expectation, 1905–09
Mixed media on paper, 193.5 x 115 cm (76 x 48 in)
• Museum of Applied Arts, Vienna

A tribute to the arts of Asia, with some reference to ancient Egypt and Byzantium, this shows the mosaic technique that Klimt had learned at the Kunstgewerbeschule. The female figure can barely be distinguished from the background.

The Stoclet Frieze: The Tree of Life, 1905–09
Mixed media on paper, 138.8 x 102 cm (54 x 40 in)
• Museum of Applied Arts, Vienna

Central to the *Stoclet Frieze*, this theme suggests the biblical Garden of Eden, the seasons, life and death and more. Its golden trunk and swirling branches were inspired by Japanese and ancient Egyptian art.

The Stoclet Frieze: Fulfilment (The Embrace), 1905–09
Mixed media on paper, 194.5 x 120.3 cm (76¾ x 42¼ in)
• © Museum of Applied Arts, Vienna

Klimt's mosaic technique here reflected his admiration of the Ravenna mosaics, with elements of Asian and Byzantine art that Adolphe Stoclet particularly admired. A man with his back turned embraces a woman.

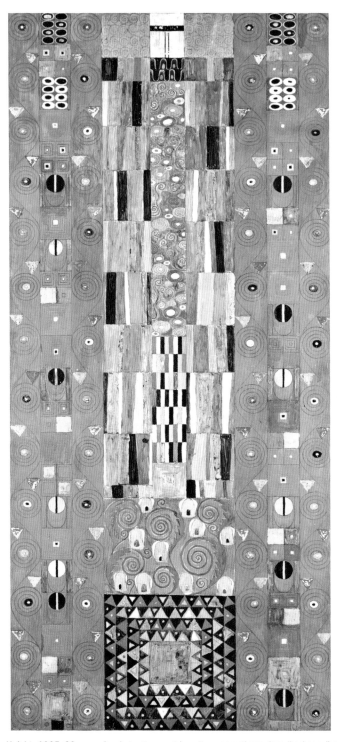

Stoclet Frieze: geometric design, or Knight, 1905–09
Mixed media on paper, 197 × 91 cm (77½ × 35¾ in)
• The Museum of Applied Arts, Vienna

An abstract geometric pattern, sometimes described as a 'knight', this panel was designed to occupy the short wall of the room, and reflects the continued use of mosaic effect.

Portrait of Adele Bloch-Bauer I, 1907
Oil, silver and gold on canvas, 138 x 138 cm (55 x 55 in)
• Kunsthistorisches Museum, Vienna

Richly embellished, this sparkling square portrait draws inspiration from ancient Egyptian, Byzantine and Mycenaean sources. The gown may allude to the myth of Juno, who scattered the eyes of Argus on to the peacock's tail.

The Kiss, 1907
Oil and gold on canvas, 180 x 180 cm (71 x 71 in)
• Kunsthistorisches Museum, Vienna

A man bends to embrace a woman. They appear as one. The symbolic circles and rectangles are offset by colourful flowers and the overall subject is of love and spirituality – and Klimt's conviction of the power of art.

Hope II, 1907–08
Oil, gold and platinum on canvas, 110.5 x 110.5 cm (43½ x 43½ in)
• Museum of Modern Art, New York

A skull can be discerned nestling against an expectant mother's ornately decorated dress. She and three other women bow their heads, probably in worship, possibly in sorrow. The entire work seems to be designed as an icon.

Danaë, 1907–08
Oil on canvas, 77 × 83 cm (30.3 × 32.7 in)
• Leopold Museum, Vienna

This symbolizes the moment when the most important god, Zeus, visited the beautiful mortal Danaë while she was imprisoned by her father, the King of Argos. Zeus is symbolized as golden rain cascading between Danaë's legs.

Judith II, 1909
Oil and gold on canvas, 178 x 48 cm (70 x 18 in)
• Galleria d'Arte Moderna Ca'Pesaro, Venice

Klimt showed this at the second Kunstschau alongside works by Matisse, Gauguin, Munch, Vuillard and Bonnard. Having just beheaded Holofernes, Judith rushes away, her hair in disarray, her embellished gown falling off her.

Landscapes: Colour & Atmosphere

Klimt painted landscapes for his own pleasure. With the appearance of colourful enamels or mosaics, they are unlike any other artists' landscapes.

After the Rain, *c.* 1898–99
Oil on canvas, 80 x 40 cm (31½ x 15¾ in)
• Österreichische Galerie Belvedere, Vienna

Painted while Klimt was working on the Faculty Paintings, the soft application of paint and restricted palette depicts a moment after rain, with chickens wandering beneath the trees. It was a relaxing change for Klimt.

Still Pond, or Reflection, 1899
Oil on canvas, 75.1 x 75.1 cm (29½ x 29½ in)
• Leopold Museum, Vienna

Klimt turned to landscape painting late in his career, after the foundation of the Vienna Secession in 1897. Landscape painting gave him relief after his work was criticized. His style here recalls Monet's atmospheric landscapes.

Farmhouse with Birch Trees, 1900
Oil on canvas, 80 x 80 cm (31½ x 31½ in)
• Österreichische Galerie Belvedere, Vienna

Adopting the Impressionist technique of short, broken brush marks, Klimt's landscape compositions focused on pattern. This entire painting is predominantly of grass with a few silver birch trunks and a glimmer of the farmhouse on the horizon.

Lake Attersee, 1900
Oil on canvas, 80.2 x 80.2 cm (31½ x 31½ in)
• Leopold Museum, Vienna

From the jetty of a small boathouse by the Flöge residence, Klimt painted this view of Lake Attersee. Focusing on the surface of the water, he applied impressionistic-style layers of harmoniously coloured brushstrokes.

Fir Forest I, 1901
Oil on canvas, 90 x 90 cm (35½ x 35½ in)
• Kamm Collection Foundation, Zug

While staying on Lake Attersee, Klimt walked through the woods at 6.00 am each day and then painted en plein air. The shallow depth of this work demonstrates how, above all, he was fascinated by shape and colour.

Beech Grove I, 1903
Oil on canvas, 100 x 100 cm (39½ x 39½ in)
• Gemäldegalerie, Dresden

The dense network of birch tree trunks and a bed of richly coloured autumn leaves appealed to Klimt's sense of pattern. As with most of his landscapes, this was a theme he painted more than once.

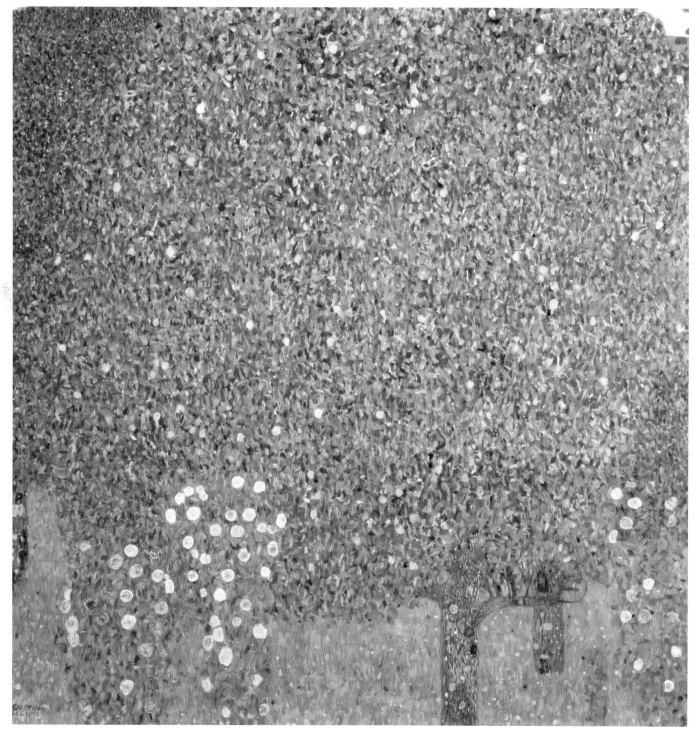

Rose Bushes under the Trees, *c.* 1905
Oil on canvas, 110 x 110 cm (43¼ x 43¼ in)
• Musée d'Orsay, Paris

Produced when Klimt was staying in Litzlberg near Lake Attersee, this work is built up with small dots and dabs of colour, creating the look of a mosaic or colourful enamel. There was no attempt to portray tonal contrast.

Orchard, or Field of Flowers, _c._ 1905
Oil on canvas, 99 x 99 cm (39 x 39 in)
• Carnegie Museum of Art, Pittsburgh

For this tranquil scene, Klimt chose an elevated viewpoint and applied paint in delicate, sensitive strokes, combining long adjacent marks and slabs of colour, creating a mosaic-like, decorative and flat appearance.

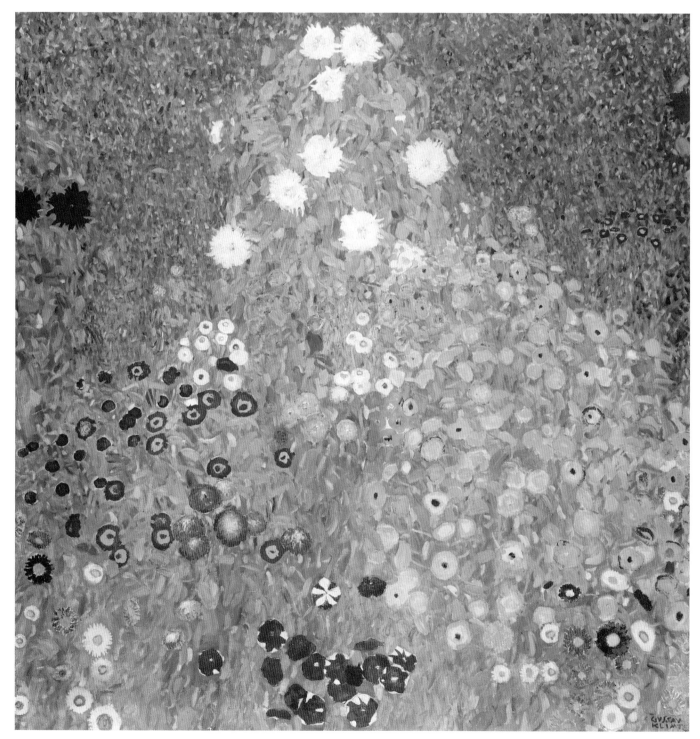

Flower Garden, or Farm Garden, 1905–07
Oil on canvas, 110 x 110 cm (43¼ x 43¼ in)
• Fondation Rau pour le Tiers-Monde, Zürich

As a complete break from his portraits and allegories, Klimt continued to explore colour, shape and composition in his landscape paintings. This close-up of flowers is lively, vibrant, unconventional and jewel-like.

Poppy Field, 1907
Oil on canvas, 110 x 110 cm (43¼ x 43¼ in)
• Österreichische Galerie Belvedere, Vienna

With a high horizon, the foreground dominates this image, creating a sense of a vast expanse of poppies. Although this subject was explored by Monet and Renoir, stylistically it is extremely different from Impressionism.

The Sunflower, 1907
Oil on canvas, 110 x 110 cm (43¼ x 43¼ in)
• Private Collection

Painted the year before he created *The Kiss*, this work was the inspiration for the latter's composition. Emilie Flöge posed in front of these sunflowers when Klimt photographed her, which probably also instigated ideas.

Schloss Kammer on Lake Attersee I, 1908
Oil on canvas, 110 x 110 cm (43¼ x 43¼ in)
• National Gallery, Prague

Overlooking the lake and almost concealed by foliage, Schloss Kammer, an eighteenth-century villa, appears tranquil, rising above the glass-like water. The painting demonstrates Klimt's delight in the abundance of nature.

Schloss Kammer on Lake Attersee II, 1909
Oil on canvas, 110 x 110 cm (43¼ x 43¼ in)
• Private Collection

A year after Klimt had painted the previous work, he painted the same subject again. Rather than depicting the reflections on the lake as before, he painted the verdant meadow in front of the castle.

Schloss Kammer on Lake Attersee III, 1910
Oil on canvas, 110 x 110 cm (43¼ x 43¼ in)
• Österreichische Galerie Belvedere, Vienna

Klimt painted this version of Schloss Kammer for his friend Adele Bloch-Bauer. He probably painted it from a boat, using a telescope. The work is more stylized than his previous two paintings of the subject.

The Park, 1910
Oil on canvas, 110.5 x 110.5 cm (43½ x 43½ in)
• Museum of Modern Art, New York

Seeking to record changes in the hours and the seasons, Klimt's painting of foliage resembles an intricate embroidery or mosaic. Recalling Seurat's pointillist style, the colours and meticulous paint application suppress any sense of depth.

Farmhouse in Upper Austria, 1911–12
Oil on canvas, 110 x 110 cm (43¼ x 43¼ in)
• Österreichische Galerie Belvedere, Vienna

The influence of both van Gogh and Toulouse-Lautrec can be seen in this painting through Klimt's undulating brushwork and depiction of contrasting textures in a flat, stylized approach. The colours also resemble a Post-Impressionist palette.

Avenue of Schloss Kammer, 1912
Oil on canvas, 110 x 110 cm (43¼ x 43¼ in)
• Österreichische Galerie Belvedere, Vienna

Reminiscent of Cézanne's compositions and the style of van Gogh, this work shows Klimt's development from an academic painter of public works to a modern artist expressing himself. Colour and decoration remain paramount.

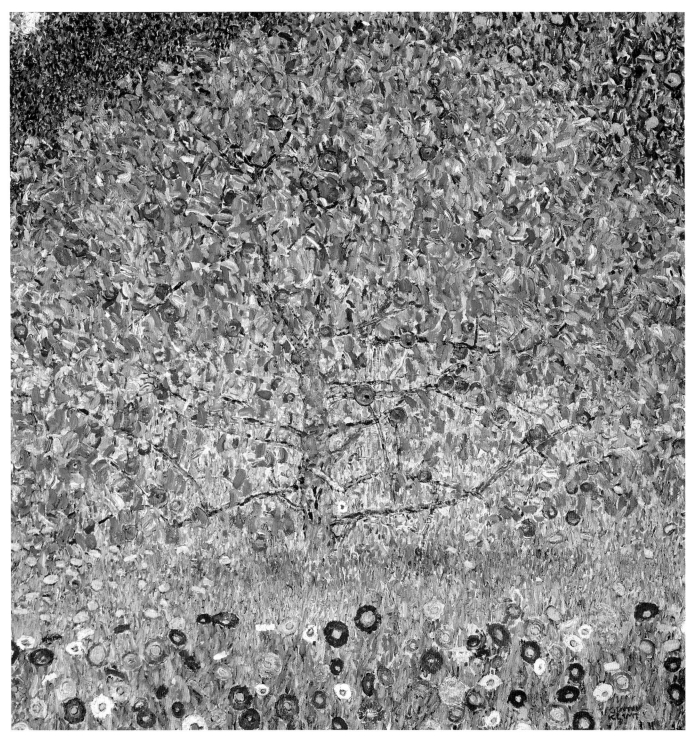

Apple Tree I, *c.* 1912
Oil on canvas, 109 x 110 cm (43 x 43¼ in)
• Private Collection

Formerly owned by Adele and Ferdinand Bloch-Bauer, this brightly coloured work seems to be bursting with happiness and nature's generosity. The small brush marks and layers of colour emit a sense of movement rare in Klimt's landscapes.

Italian Garden, 1913
Oil on canvas, 110 x 110 cm (43¼ x 43¼ in)
• Kamm Collection Foundation, Zug

For 15 days during July and August 1913, Klimt spent the summer with friends in Italy on Lake Garda. He painted this vibrant image in the gardens of Albergo Morandi, where they were staying.

Malcesine on Lake Garda, 1913
Oil on canvas, 110 x 110 cm (43¼ x 43¼ in) • Destroyed by retreating
German forces in 1945

During the two weeks that Klimt spent in Italy on Lake Garda during 1913, he painted three works. This colourful and decorative painting that seems to have taken a leap into modernity is one of them. Destroyed by retreating German forces in 1945.

Church in Cassone, 1913
Oil on canvas, 110 x 110 cm (43¼ x 43¼ in)
• Private Collection

One of three works that Klimt painted when staying in Italy near Lake Garda, this was painted from Malcesine, and Klimt used a telescope in his quest to create a harmonious composition of vegetation, architecture and water.

Forester's House in Weissenbach I, *c.* **1914**
Oil on canvas, 110 x 110 cm (43¼ x 43¼ in)
• Private Collection

Integrating architectural elements into natural scenes fascinated Klimt and is something he tackled often while in Attersee. The summer foliage helped soften the building's lines. He is not known to have painted any winter landscapes.

Forester's House in Weissenbach II, 1914
Oil on canvas, 110 x 110 cm (43¼ x 43¼ in)
• Private Collection

During the summer of 1914, when Austria declared war on Serbia, Klimt lived in this house. Cut off from the troubles, he painted in a style strongly influenced by van Gogh, creating a flat, illustrative image.

Litzlberg on Lake Attersee, 1915
Oil on canvas, 110 x 110 cm (43¼ x 43¼ in)
• Private Collection

An eyewitness recalled seeing Klimt at work: 'In Litzlberg – the village lies across the lake from Kammer – we saw a man in a large meadow in front of an easel, in spite of the drizzle and cold, painting.'

Houses in Unterach on Lake Attersee, 1916
Oil on canvas, 110 x 110 cm (43¼ x 43¼ in)
• Private Collection

Bought by Adele and Ferdinand Bloch-Bauer, this painting shows where Klimt sought solace and spent most of the First World War years. Even in this peaceful place, he was aware of the horrors that were occurring across Europe.

Church in Unterach on Lake Attersee, c. 1916
Oil on canvas, 110 x 110 cm (43¼ x 43¼ in)
• Private Collection

Painted from the little village of Weissenbach, Klimt used binoculars across Lake Attersee to catch the details of this view. Perspective has been abandoned in favour of shapes, textures and colours, creating a patchwork-like effect.

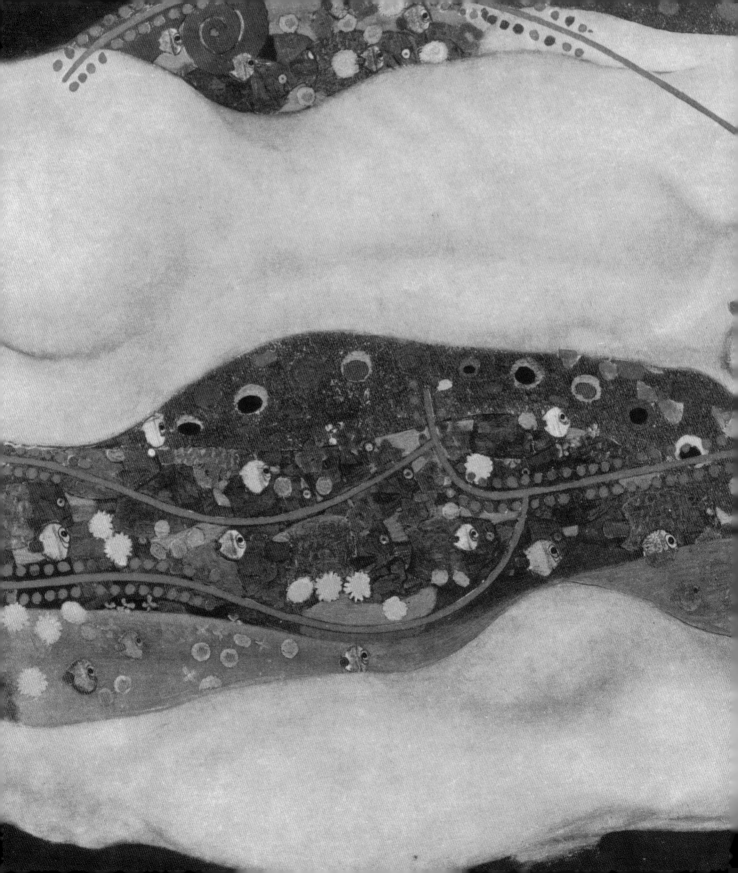

Portraits & Later Style

As well as various images of femininity, including pregnancy, motherhood and ageing, Klimt painted numerous portraits of society women. His later work became particularly expressive and vibrant.

Portrait of Joseph Pembauer, 1890
Canvas and frame painted in oil and gold, 69 x 55 cm (27 x 22 in)
• Tyrolean Provincial Museum, Innsbruck

An almost photographic likeness, this portrait of the pianist and teacher was painted soon after *Auditorium in the Old Burgtheater* (*see* page 33), and continues the same meticulous details and realism the public admired.

Actor Josef Lewinsky as Carlos, 1895
Oil on canvas, 64 x 44 cm (25 x 17 in)
• Österreichische Galerie Belvedere, Vienna

In 1894, Klimt was commissioned to paint an actor in a stage role. He chose Josef Lewinsky as Don Carlos in Goethe's *Clavigo*, which was extremely successful and repeated every year at the Burgtheater.

Study of the Head of a Blind Man, _c._ 1896–98
Oil on canvas, 67 x 53 cm (26 x 21 in)
• Private Collection

Klimt made two studies of this man, who was probably paid to pose for him. This version was exhibited at the first Secessionist exhibition. Klimt's spontaneous and expressive application was inspirational for many younger artists.

Portrait of Sonja Knips, 1898
Oil on canvas, 145 x 145 cm (57 x 57 in)
• Österreichische Galerie Belvedere, Vienna

Thoughtful or impatient? Klimt's portrait of his friend Sonja Knips just after her marriage to the industrial tycoon Anton Knips seems to radiate with a rosy glow. She was one of the first society ladies he painted.

Portrait of Helene Klimt, 1898
Oil on card, 60 x 40 cm (23 x 15¾ in)
• Private Collection

This elegant portrait is of Klimt's six-year-old niece, daughter of his late brother Ernst. After Ernst's death, Klimt became Helene's legal guardian. This shows the compositional and stylistic influence of J.A.M. Whistler.

Schubert at the Piano, 1899
Oil on canvas, 150 x 200 cm (59 x 78¾ in)
• Destroyed by retreating German forces in 1945

The Greek industrialist Nikolaus Dumba particularly admired Franz Schubert, and Klimt painted this for him. The writer and critic Hermann Bahr (1863-1934) wrote: 'Klimt's Schubert is the finest painting ever done by an Austrian.' Destroyed by retreating German forces in 1945.

Portrait of Serena Lederer, 1899
Oil on canvas, 188 x 83 cm (74 x 32 in)
• Metropolitan Museum of Art, New York

Married to the industrialist August Lederer, Serena is believed to have commissioned this herself. The diaphanous white dress against the white background is evocative of the work of Whistler, whom Klimt admired.

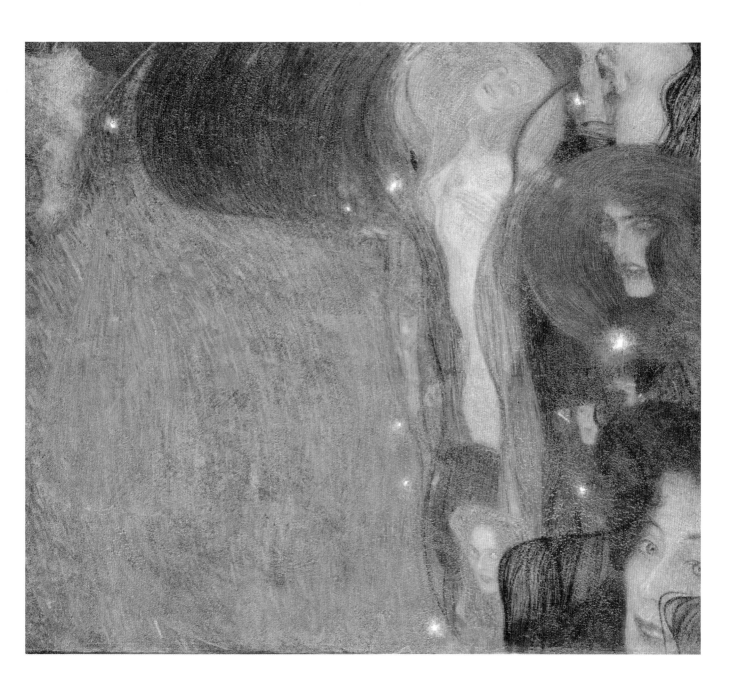

Will-o'-the-Wisp, or Irrlichter, 1903
Oil on board laid down on canvas, 52 x 59.5 cm (20½ x 23½ in)
• Private Collection

This work was lost until 1978. Here, Klimt explores the will-o'-the-wisp, a flame-like phosphorescent light created by gases from decaying plants in marshes. Foolish travellers who tried to follow the light were led to their doom.

Portrait of Hermine Gallia, 1904
Oil on canvas, 170.5 x 96.5 cm (67 x 38 in)
• The National Gallery, London

In 1893, Hermine Hamburger married her uncle, Moritz Gallia, a government adviser who was a patron of the arts. Hermine stands on a conventionally patterned carpet against a plain background, wearing a dress designed by Klimt.

Portrait of Margaret Stonborough-Wittgenstein, 1905
Oil on canvas, 180 x 90 cm (70 x 35½in)
• Neue Pinakothek, Munich

Margaret Wittgenstein was a member of a wealthy Viennese family who patronized the arts. On the occasion of her marriage to the wealthy American Jerome Stonborough, Margaret's father paid Klimt to paint this portrait of her.

Portrait of Fritza Riedler, 1906
Oil on canvas, 153 x 133 cm (60¼ x 52 in)
• Kunsthistorisches Museum, Vienna

One of Klimt's many portraits of fashionable, wealthy Viennese women, this shows the influence of Velázquez's seventeenth-century portraits of Spanish royal ladies. It also typifies Klimt's elegant response to Art Nouveau.

Water Serpents II, 1907
Oil on canvas, 80 x 145 cm (31½ x 57 in) • Private Collection

Swimming naked, their hair entwined with plants and embellished with gold leaf, Klimt's women are lesbians – a subject that would have shocked Viennese society but for the work's beauty.

Lady with Hat and Feather Boa, 1909
Oil on canvas, 69 x 55 cm (27 x 21 in)
• Private Collection

The developing Expressionist styles of Egon Schiele and Oskar Kokoschka inspired Klimt to abandon his 'Golden Phase'. Clearly also following elements of Toulouse-Lautrec's style, this painting was not commissioned and the woman is unidentified.

The Black Feather Hat, 1910
Oil on canvas, 79 x 63 cm (31 x 25 in)
• Private Collection

Inspired by the Baroque styles of van Dyck and Franz Hals, this portrait also shows the influence of Toulouse-Lautrec, and demonstrates Klimt's abandonment of gold and change of style after he had visited Paris in 1909.

Death and Life, 1910 (reworked 1915)
Oil on canvas, 178 x 198 cm (70 x 78 in)
• Leopold Collection, Vienna

Death, or the Grim Reaper, watches the intertwined figures of all generations. They represent the circle of life, and the image shows that, while Death can take individuals, humanity as a whole will always evade him.

Farm (or Cottage) Garden with Crucifix, 1911–12
Oil on canvas, 110 x 110 cm (43¼ x 43¼ in)
• Destroyed by retreating German forces in 1945

Rendered as an intricate embroidery, this was the first of a group of works painted by Klimt using more obvious, linear marks than previously. The crucifix was located near Lake Attersee, where Klimt saw it on his walks. Destroyed by retreating German forces in 1945.

Miss Ria Munk on her Deathbed, 1912
Oil on canvas, 50 x 50.5 cm (19 x 19¾ in)
• Private Collection

Ria Munk was the niece of Serena Lederer, daughter of Alexander and Aranka Munk. At 23 years old, she shot herself after an unhappy love affair. Her grief-stricken parents commissioned Klimt to paint posthumous portraits of her.

Portrait of Mäda Primavesi, 1912
Oil on canvas, 150 x 110 cm (59 x 43¼ in)
• The Metropolitan Museum of Art, New York

The nine-year-old daughter of banker and industrialist Otto Primavesi, one of the financial backers of the Vienna Werkstätte, and actress Eugenia Primavesi, Mäda seems quite sophisticated here. Cheerful decorations complement the image.

Portrait of Adele Bloch-Bauer II, 1912
Oil on canvas, 190 x 120 cm (75 x 47¼ in)
• Private Collection

Ferdinand and Adele Bloch-Bauer commissioned Klimt regularly, and Adele was one of only a couple of sitters who had her portrait painted by him more than once. Although highly decorative, this contrasts with the elaborate style of his earlier portrait of Adele.

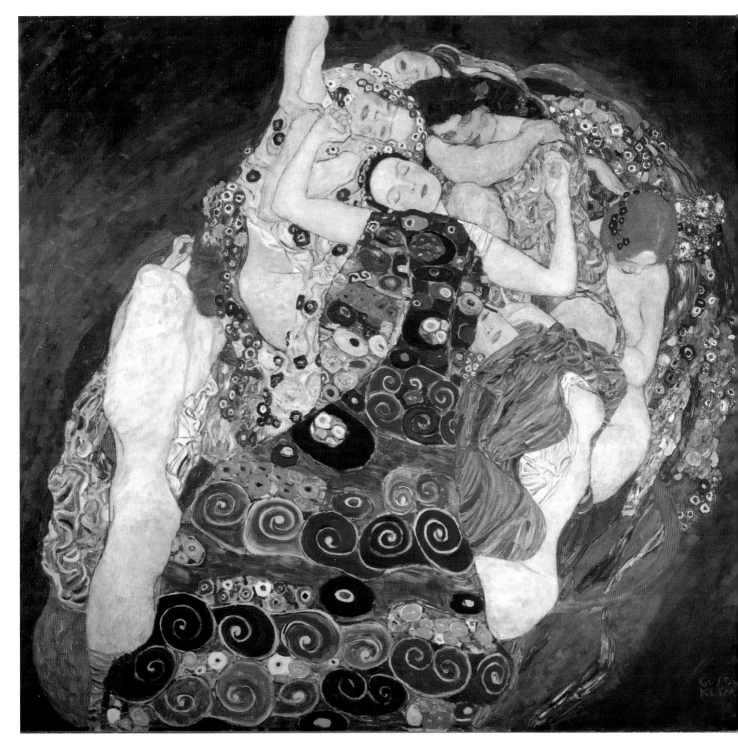

The Virgin, 1912–13
Oil on canvas, 190 x 200 cm (74¾ x 78¾ in)
• National Gallery, Prague

Either sleeping or just awakening, the seven women are entwined with each other, flowers and patterns.
The central figure is the Virgin, the other six are of different ages, representing stages in a woman's life.

Portrait of Eugenia Primavesi, *c.* 1913–14
Oil on canvas, 140 x 80 cm (55 x 31½ in)
• Private Collection

Exploding with life and colour, this painting is filled with energy despite the subject's seated pose. Eugenia Primavesi was married to the industrialist Otto Primavesi, and had a strong influence over the choice of art he commissioned.

Portrait of Baroness Elisabeth Bachofen-Echt, *c.* **1914**
Oil on canvas, 180 × 126 cm (70 x 49 in)
• Private Collection

Elisabeth Bachofen-Echt, Serena Lederer's daughter, is an example of Klimt's evolving style and of women's fashions. This painting features darker colours than his previous works, and Japanese-style motifs, including birds, animals and figures.

Portrait of Friederike Maria Beer, 1916
Oil on canvas, 168 x 130 cm (66 x 51¼ in)
• Tel Aviv Museum of Art, Mizne-Blumental Collection

A wealthy Viennese woman, Friederike Maria Beer commissioned Klimt to paint her portrait. She wore a hand-painted silk dress from the Vienna Werkstätte that she called 'my Klimt dress'. Klimt also explored Japanese art in the painting.

Portrait of a Young Woman, 1916–17
Oil on canvas, 60 x 55 cm (23 x 21 in)
• Galleria d'Arte Moderna, Piacenza

In a lively style, Klimt's portrait of this unknown young woman shows the influence of several other painting methods. In particular, the bright colours and sketchy application resemble Alexei von Jawlensky's Expressionist style.

Women Friends, 1916–17
Oil on canvas, 99 x 99 cm (39 x 39 in)
• Destroyed by retreating German forces in 1945

August Lederer collected Klimt's work, but many were destroyed when German soldiers set fire to his home at the end of the Second World War. This ambiguous painting was one of them; of it only studies and photographs remain.

Portrait of Ria Munk III (unfinished), 1917–18
Oil on canvas, 180 x 128 cm (70 x 50 in)
• Private Collection

The third and final painting of Ria Munk, who had committed suicide in 1912, this was unfinished at the time of Klimt's death. It reveals his working methods of drawing lightly to allow for any later changes.

The Bride (unfinished), 1917–18
Oil on canvas, 165 x 191 cm (65 x 75¼ in)
• Private Collection

This unfinished work was in Klimt's studio when he died. Over the drawn, naked figures, he had started to paint clothes of symbolic ornamental shapes. His earlier gold was now replaced with dazzling colours.

Portrait of Johanna Staude (unfinished), 1917–18
Oil on canvas, 70 x 50 cm (27½ x 19 in)
• Österreichische Galerie Belvedere, Vienna

Beginning to display an almost savage exoticism, this portrait of Johanna Staude is one of Klimt's last portraits, and left unfinished at his death. The simple composition is offset by the contrasting, striking colours.

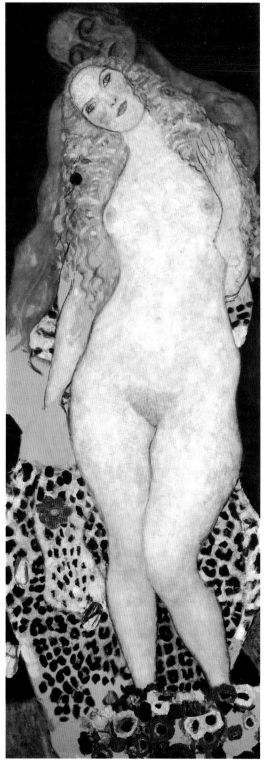

Adam and Eve (unfinished), 1917
Oil on canvas, 173 x 60 cm (68 x 23 in)
• Österreichische Galerie Belvedere, Vienna

In bright and light colours, Eve is the main figure here, while Adam in the background is darker-skinned and seems to be there simply to contrast with Eve and set off her milky white skin.

Lady with Fan, 1917
Oil on canvas, 100 x 100 cm (39½ x 39½ in)
• Private Collection

In one of Klimt's last completed works, the lady in a kimono is not known, but the soft style is reminiscent of the Oriental art that was hugely popular with contemporary artists and designers.

Indexes

Index of Works

General Index

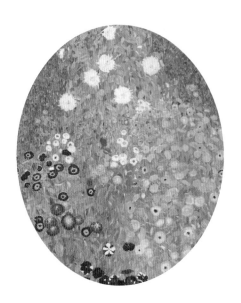

Masterpieces of Art

FLAME TREE PUBLISHING

A new series of carefully curated print and digital books covering the world's greatest art, artists and art movements.

If you enjoyed this book please sign up for updates, information and offers on further titles in this series at

blog.flametreepublishing.com/art-of-fine-gifts/